RED AND PURPLE

HIKING BOOTS

Donna Billings' courage and determination to take multiple risks despite the "better judgment" of various naysayers inspires the reader to break with her old life patterns and dive into a totally new existence. This book is the next best thing to having a personal coach.

~ Joan Anderson, author, *A Year by the Sea*

Just when you thought a coach never reveals her own story, Donna Billings breaks her silence and shares her own life-changing moments and her best coaching techniques. What a gift!

~ Deborah Godfrey Muck, Ubika Coaching

Travel alongside this wise and adventurous woman on her later-life journey and amazingly discover more of yourself in the process!

~ Nina El-Tobgy, Retail Owner and Fellow Life Traveler

Donna Billings has the wisdom of years, and the sagacity to not take herself too seriously. A delightful read!

~ Andrea Sigetich, author, *Play to Your Strengths*

Donna's book is a great story of how one woman redefined herself beginning in her older years. As a talented coach, Donna mines her story for lessons that she shares with others. A truly inspirational read.

~ Dr. Susan Merrie English, Life Coach

This book is for anyone who has felt the call of a dream while those around her slept. The dreams speak while angels speak encouragement and demons whisper and sometimes shout their doubts and criticism. Donna is a docent for everyone on the Journey of Becoming.

~ Ron Campbell, President, Center for Leadership Studies

Read this book and you will have made a giant deposit in your self-worth account!

~ Carolyn Lyle, EEO Director, Defense Security Service

Red and Purple Hiking Boots tells the story of a journey—both inner and outer—and how one inspires and feeds the other. Through her own stories and adventures, Donna shows that courage is not the lack of fear, but action in spite of it. She lets all of us know there is more learning and growing ahead, no matter our age! Let her journey inspire your own.

~ Dr. Michael Forlenza, Leadership Development Coach

Donna Billings is the Mother of coaching innovation in Pittsburgh.

~ Sharon Eakes, co-author, *Liberating Greatness*

RED AND PURPLE

HIKING BOOTS

An ^ Woman's Trek to "It's Never too Late"

Older

Donna R. Billings, MBE, CPPC, PCC
Professional Certified Coach

This book was written and published in partnership with inCredible Messages, LP
www.inCredibleMessages.com

Disclaimer: This memoir and coaching book covers a very specific time in my life. In some places, I have changed the names and identifying characteristics to protect those who have asked to remain private. Also, in several places I have condensed several events or people to more fully make a point.

To contact the author, Donna Billings, visit
Websites .... : www.DonnaBillingsCoach.com
www.RedAndPurpleHikingBoots.com
Linked in .... : http://www.linkedin.com/pub/donna-billings/1/a4/8b5
Facebook... : Donna Billings
Twitter........ : Donna Billings@billings_donna

To contact the publisher, inCredible Messages Press, visit
www.inCredibleMessages.com

Printed in the United States of America

ISBN 978-0-9889266-2-2 Paperback
ISBN 978-0-9889266-3-9 e-Book

-Memoir   -Self Help

Book Coaching ....: Bonnie Budzowski, inCredible Messages, LP
Editing ....: inCredible Messages, LP
Interior Design...........: inCredible Messages, LP
Cover Artwork............: Kristen McMenamin and Ryan Landis
Cover Design.............: Bobbie Fox, Bobbie Fox, Inc.
Author Photograph ....: Doug Ellis Photography

July 2013

Corrin –
   Let this book inspire
you.

   Donna Billings

Donna trekking in Death Valley National Park

DEDICATION

For all women in the world who are ready to step into their power and soar

Acknowledgments

To my phenomenal son, Jamie. Together we made your Dad's last years worthwhile and as peaceful as we could. Through this entire journey you have been here for me; together we partnered to coordinate travel schedules so one of us was always nearby for your Dad. I knew I could count on you to lend a helping hand or just a shoulder to cry on when needed. I am so proud of you, my son and my friend.

To my niece, Kristen McMenamin, who stepped way outside her comfort zone and worked through fears of rejection to design this book cover. I love what you did with my hiking boots. Thank you.

To my grandnephew, Ryan Landis, who also helped with the book cover. I loved that we could keep this within our creative family.

To Bonnie Budzowski, my book coach, who patiently urged me over a period of 10 years to write this book. Without your gently worded notes, phone calls—and yes—reprimands, this book would still be hidden in my many journals. Your skills are exceptional.

To my wonderful support group of women: Nina, Arlene, Ann, Kaaren, Andrea, the Wild Women, Chris, Danielle, Paulette, and others who touched my life over the past 15 years—you were the catalysts that helped sustain my equilibrium when I thought I couldn't stand one more day.

To all my clients, colleagues, and friends who convinced me that my stories were worth writing about.

To Don, who in spite of our turbulent last years together, loved me unequivocally and died being proud of all I had accomplished. Thank you for your deep love and devotion. I think you'd approve of and love reading this book.

Finally, to Glenn. If not now, when?

The original Wild Women
Crater Lake National Park
Charlene, Andrea, Donna, Jan, Lois, Linda, Marion

Donna kayaking with Glenn
Alaska

Jamie wearing a shirt to support St. Baldrick's Foundation efforts for children with cancer

Wild Women
Glacier National Park
Front: Linda, Jan
Rear: Carol, Lois, Donna, Charlene, Marion, Andrea

Don at a time of relative
health
Taos, New Mexico

Donna and Ann
Machu Picchu

Donna overcoming a fear of heights
North Rim of the Grand Canyon

Donna posing with a
cairn (guidepost)
Death Valley National
Park

CONTENTS

CHAPTER 1

WON'T YOU TRAVEL WITH ME?

> *Life isn't simple. But the beauty of it is, you can always start over. It'll get easier.*
>
> ~ Alacia Bessette

THE CLIMBING GUIDES FOR OUR GROUP, Shay and Mario, kept saying, "Eat, eat your carbs. Drink, drink," but I couldn't do either. The food just would not go down. On the upward climb, I struggled, not only to eat and drink but also to breathe. For hours, I was convinced I could go no farther.

Sweating and struggling, I couldn't imagine why, at age 62, I had decided to climb Machu Picchu, with a height of nearly 15,000 feet. Why would I think I could accomplish such a thing with no hiking experience and no conditioning?

What kind of illusions was I harboring? The time in my life for this kind of adventure was long past. I had missed the opportunity of youth, and there was no way now I could live out my dreams of unique hiking adventures. I wanted nothing more than to climb back down the mountain and feel sorry for myself.

No matter my misery, there was no easy, fast path down the mountain, so I was forced to continue to hike slowly. That night, as I lay in my tent exhausted, I decided that my mental perspective was holding me back. I promised myself that on the following day, when we climbed the highest point over Dead Woman's Pass, I was going to think positively and focus on making it to camp that evening.

The following day, however, I was overcome with altitude sickness, even though my companion and I had arrived at the starting point several days early to allow time to adjust. Altitude sickness includes symptoms of drowsiness, general malaise and weakness, as well as headache, insomnia, persistent rapid pulse, nausea, and vomiting.

As I trudged forward one step at a time, a mantra reverberated in my brain, "I got to get off this mountain. I got to get off this mountain." With each reverberation, I became more and more scared.

The guides pushed their water, and I drank the little I could, but I was unable to urinate and I couldn't eat. The guides gave me cocaine leaves to chew, a stimulant.

As we crossed Dead Woman's Pass, the highest point, the mantra changed its refrain, "Not going to make it. Not going to make it." I began to weave. I could no longer drink. I vomited. The guides gave me oxygen.

"I'm not going to make it. I'm not going to make it."

Shay and Mario positioned themselves, one on each side of me. I have no memory of coming over the pass, the most beautiful part of the hike. When we got to camp—dead last, the guides put me into a tent and monitored me in my stupor. Shay slept in my tent that night to keep watch. I missed the experience of the camp surroundings entirely, complete with springs and waterfalls.

On the third day, I woke up weary but determined. Intimidated by altitude sickness but unwilling to give up, I renewed my resolve to make it to camp that day and have fun in the process. I deliberately changed my mantra to, "I can do this. I can do this."

Shay and Mario continued to hike with me as everyone else went ahead. I remember a member of our group, a beautiful 24-year-old Amazon-looking woman from California, running down the mountain while I limped my way along.

At one point, Shay, Mario, and I somehow forgot the safety protocol. Rather than me hiking against the side of the mountain with a guide along the edge, I was on the edge. The next thing I knew, I fell, head first, over the side of the mountain into a pool of moss. Shay and Mario had to pull me out by my feet. In the process, I lost my glasses.

We still had eight hours left, during which we were descending steps. The steps were so steep that they seemed nearly vertical to me. Descending those steps under normal circumstances would have been strenuous. In my condition, the task seemed impossible.

The guides resumed their posts on either side of me. I took one step at a time. I adjusted the mantra in my head, "I can do this. One step and drop. I can do this. One step and drop." I hung onto my hiking poles and relied on Shay and Mario to guide me to camp.

By the time I reached camp, my legs refused to stand straight. After my fall off the mountain and my less than elegant entrance into camp, the group gave me the nickname "Rubber Legs Billings." While every ounce of my body ached, I was at least able to join in the laughter at my expense.

Barely able to walk, however, I was preoccupied with how I was ever going to be able to hike the four hours into the Machu

Picchu ruins at dawn on the following day. To cover the additional distance, we'd be hiking in the dark.

On day four, I awoke at 3:30 a.m., feeling like a million bucks. I pulled on my hiking boots and surprised myself and everyone else by keeping up with the group as we hiked to Sun Gate. Granted, I had to crawl up a series of 30 steps at the end, but I made it! The feeling was amazing—I had pushed myself beyond what I thought was my limit, and I made it! The mantra in my head that day was, "I made it. I made it. I can't believe I made it!"

To say the Machu Picchu hike was transforming would be to make the biggest understatement of my life. I returned home with the confidence to accomplish anything I set out to do, more confidence than I had gained in the first 62 years of my life. I had battled a mountain and won. This was the beginning of an older woman's climb to "it's never too late."

At the time of this writing, my Machu Picchu adventure is ten years past. During the intervening years, I've climbed a number of mountains and enjoyed adventures in remote parts of the world as well as in many national parks within the United States. At 72, I'm still hiking, kayaking, and taking risks. It turns out it was not too late at all to live my dreams.

My journey from Machu Picchu to here was definitely not easy. I had to fight and struggle to travel at all, given that my husband, Don, needed my care until he died recently. In addition, the assumptions and voices in my head said:

"Your place is home with your husband."

"A woman your age needs security, not adventure."

"You have no right to take time and money for yourself."

My own intuition and my victory over Machu Picchu had something different to say, and I was determined to listen.

I made a decision to be faithful to Don and care for him. At the same time, I made a decision to live life on my own terms, to take time for myself and pursue my own dreams. As is the case with most women, my life was full of push and pull.

During these years, I supported myself as a certified professional coach, working with clients to achieve their goals and to smoothly transition from one season of life to another. In addition, as founder of Duquesne University's Professional Coach Certification Program, I worked with many aspiring coaches.

Over the past 10 years, my clients and students asked me repeatedly to tell my story. And now I am. As a coach, however, I'm profoundly interested in how my story will interact with yours. I've designed this book so my story will be a starting point for you to reflect upon your own, so my vision will be an example as you contemplate yours, and so my path will be one option as you consider your own path.

HOW TO USE THIS BOOK

If you are someone who struggles with the push and pull in your life, this book is for you. If you are someone who wants to live life to the fullest, this book is for you. If you are someone who feels hemmed in by life's roles and circumstances, this book is for you. And if you are someone who is in transition from one season of life to another, this book is for you.

As I've told my story, I've tried to be authentic about my struggles, doubts, and insecurities as well as my solutions and victories. This book is a safe place, devoid of judgment or guilt.

While each chapter pulls back the curtain on a portion of my story, beginning in my mid-50s, it doesn't stop there. Following each story, you'll find a section called, "From My Life to Yours." This section will briefly explore some of the themes found in that portion of my story.

In the final section of each chapter, you'll find a series of exercises designed to guide you to reflect on how the themes operate in your life. The exercises will guide you to articulate your dreams, formulate a vision, explore the assumptions that hold you back, and take action to ensure your vision becomes reality. In many ways, the power in this book lay in the exercises, as I've chosen ones I've used successfully with clients over the years.

I recommend that you purchase an attractive journal to use as you work your way through the book. This will allow you to keep all your notes in one place and to refer to them as a unit in the future. I also recommend that you schedule the time and space you'll need to give the exercises your complete attention.

Invest in yourself because you are worth it. Invest in yourself because your future depends on it. May my story inspire you to fully embrace your own.

CHAPTER 2

NICARAGUA-SANDINISTAS AND HOWLING MONKEYS

> *Courage is being scared to death but saddling up anyway.*
>
> ~John Wayne

I WOULD HAVE NEVER MADE THAT TRIP TO Machu Picchu if it hadn't been for my son, Jamie. Recently out of college, Jamie had completed roughly 1 year of his 2-1/2-year term in Nicaragua with the Peace Corps. In these days before Skype, I was longing to see my son, and I began to consider visiting him. I was 55 when I was overcome with the urge to travel to Nicaragua. Jamie was 23 and my husband, Don, was 74.

At the time, I had been out of the United States only once, and never to a third-world country. Nicaragua was full of unrest, and yet I felt drawn to go. I wanted to see Jamie, but I also felt a sense of adventure rising within. I wanted to see something outside of my experience, smell exotic air, and break free from bonds I hadn't known were holding me back.

When I expressed my plans to Don, he responded with alarm. Every time we talked about it, Don expressed his litany of concerns:

"There's a war going on down there."

"It's a third-world country."

"You'll get malaria."

"You don't speak the language."

"You'll be robbed."

It was no surprise that Don resisted my trip. Nineteen years my senior, Don had long since retired from a successful career, first as a professor of classical English at Case Western Reserve, and then as a marketing and sales professional for a business publishing house. He had a photographic memory and a penchant for perfectionism that turned out to be both a blessing and a curse.

Don's considerable mental abilities had made him successful. I had been attracted to an intelligent, sophisticated, and romantic person. We had 15 good years together before Don's drive for perfectionism came to dominate his whole personality. In retirement, Don tried a few things but never found an interest at which he could be perfect. Thus, he came to spend his retirement sitting in a chair, reading books, and watching TV. Jamie and I became increasingly distant from Don.

At the time, I was living a small, constrained life, but I didn't know it. In fact, I thought I was living a responsible and successful life. As Senior Manager of Training and Organizational Development at a major corporation, I was proud of what I had accomplished. In a high-pressure environment, I was running two distinct departments and managing aggressive project timelines.

On the home front, I was married to a man who was 19 years my senior. I had accepted the life and role of wife to an older man who expected perfection in everything. Hypercritical of himself, Don was also hypercritical of Jamie and me. At times, our home environment seemed unbearable. In fact, when Jamie was 15, I told my son I had decided to leave his dad and get an apartment. Apart from my own pain of being constantly criticized, I couldn't bear to see Jamie beaten down.

Jamie countered with a decision to stay with Dad—because he didn't believe I was strong enough to stick with my decision. I stayed put but began the process of building strength and separating my life and space from my husband. I made a silent vow that I would become strong enough to stand on my own two feet.

Once Jamie graduated from college, I put the house on the market, once again planning to leave. It took three years for the house to sell, and once again, I stayed with Don. Together, we moved into a townhouse.

I stayed with my husband even though I didn't want to. I didn't feel financially secure enough to be on my own. More importantly, unquestioned values and assumptions about marriage kept me bound. As a member of the baby boomer generation, I never questioned the assumption that a marriage vow was forever, even when the marriage no longer worked.

While Don's reaction to my proposed trip to Nicaragua was predictable, I didn't expect a similar intense reaction from my colleagues at work. My boss said, "You can't take off from work now; there's a crisis looming and we need your leadership." I no longer remember the crisis, but I do remember I was spearheading a major project on succession planning and leadership development. The timeline was aggressive, and there wasn't "room" for me to leave the country.

Both Don and my boss had reasonable points of view. I knew this. Their words were ones I might have said myself to some other middle-aged woman who proposed to travel alone to a war-torn third-world country. While one part of me was ready to agree with my detractors, another part, deep inside, knew I was running out of time to fulfill a vague longing, to satisfy a hunger I carried within. This part of me was seeking a unique adventure and begging to be unleashed.

Struggling with my good sense, my responsibilities, and the resistance of those surrounding me, I didn't sleep well for a number of weeks. My longing for adventure refused to be silenced. My desire to see Jamie persisted. It tormented me, rebelling against my common sense. One morning I got up and acted before I had a chance to hesitate. I sent a note to Jamie, saying, "I'm coming. When is the best time?"

I made airplane reservations and said to myself, "There, it's done. I can't go back." I visited the doctor to see what I needed to do to prepare for the trip, stepping over my fears and ignoring my urge to please others.

Even with the decision made to travel, the next six months were rife with doubts and challenges. The anti-malarial tablets gave me out-of-body dreams. I dreamed I was floating in space with my head blown up like a balloon. I'd float, reflecting on my life—events, people, and experiences. I'd wake up disoriented. Throughout the day, I'd say nonsensical things or begin to laugh for no reason. I was disoriented like this for a full six weeks.

As the travel date approached, I was sometimes scared to death; at other times, I couldn't wait to leave. Often, I experienced both emotions simultaneously. I found myself delivering words of calm to those around me while wondering if I was embarking on a crazy-lady plan.

Don was angry about my decision, and for a while, he badgered me. Eventually he went silent and expressed his disapproval in small, irritating ways. I drew on my courage to stick to my decision, all the while battling my own fears, "What if he is right? Why am I doing this? I must be crazy for taking this risk."

The day of my departure, I stepped through all my fears and flew with confidence from Pittsburgh to Miami, the first leg of the trip. When I boarded the plane owned by Nico Air, however, an unsettling fear boarded with me. The plane did not fit any definition of modern, and no one on the plane spoke English.

When the plane landed in Nicaragua, everyone clapped. When I mentioned this interesting custom to Jamie, he explained that the passengers had clapped because they were thankful the plane had landed safely. I found this to be unsettling, since I needed to fly on that same plane out of Nicaragua.

Stepping off the plane, I was both elated and scared to death. While it was fantastic to see and touch my son, I didn't speak the language chattered all around me. Guards with AK47 rifles made the whole scene surreal and menacing. Since I was a tourist, I had to go through customs without Jamie. Was I in the right lane? Where was I supposed to go? What was I supposed to do?

Finally, Jamie was able to retrieve me and usher me into the worst looking pickup truck I had ever seen. I rode in the cab with the driver, who smiled a lot but spoke no English. Jamie rode in the open back so the luggage wouldn't get stolen. We rode roughly an hour to Jamie's host family's abode, a shack in the country. Jamie lived in a chicken coop off the shack.

Showing me to a bed with netting, Jamie cautioned, "Make sure the netting is closed. If something does crawl on you, lie still and it will go away." Regarding the outhouse, Jamie said, "Don't worry. The maid cleaned out all the tarantulas this morning."

Such was my home for the next 10 days. Washing my clothing in the family well, sweating my way through Central American heat, and struggling to understand the language around me, I had emotional peaks and valleys. This wasn't an ideal vacation, but I was with Jamie. I had made a decision for myself and accomplished something far outside my comfort zone.

My time here with Jamie involved a complete reversal of roles. I was completely dependent on MY CHILD for my safety. In this environment, my son was strong, confident, and competent—no longer a child at all. We talked for hours and he made sure I had everything I needed.

Jamie surprised me one day by taking me on a trip to a beautiful coffee plantation. Deep in the northern part of the country, wild orchids, howling monkeys, and the wonderful smell of roasting coffee surrounded the plantation. As we traveled nearly nine hours via run-down school buses and taxis without doors, Jamie became my trusted guide, especially when we were in danger of being robbed by Sandinistas with AK47 rifles.

"Mom," said Jamie, "If we have an encounter with the Sandinistas, just give them what they want, and they will leave us alone. We'll be fine."

"Well," I thought with resignation, "I'm here now. There's no turning back." We did in fact encounter a harrowing moment when several banditos with guns approached our bus. Luckily, our bus driver took off before the banditos were able to board, so we were just fine.

Once we arrived, a walk in the rain forest and coffee plantation made all the doubts, struggles, and dangers pale in comparison. Butterflies the size of birds and howling monkeys are still vivid to me, even now, over a decade later. Nothing can compare with swimming in the ocean and eating fish caught and cooked while we played in the water.

That night, dining at the coffee plantation lodge with people of multiple nationalities, I realized Jamie was carrying the conversation, animated and with a sparkle in his eye. Son and mother were equals in an international social situation. I had done my job well.

Getting off the plane on my return trip to Pittsburgh, I was a different middle-aged woman than the one who had left just 10 days before. A sense of power, pride, and accomplishment seemed to fill every bone and every pore. What's more, I had tasted adventure travel; I had experienced a sense of awe and wonder (and fear) beyond my wildest dreams. That vague longing I'd carried inside was now clear. I wanted to travel. I WOULD travel. I was starved for travel. I was starved for the exhilaration, the fear, and the awe of unique adventure travel. As I collected my luggage and made my way home, the meaning of boredom took on a completely new dimension.

> *Cautious, careful people, always casting about to preserve their reputations . . . can never effect a reform.*
> ~ Susan B. Anthony

PRINCIPLES TO PROPEL YOU FORWARD

1. Unexplored fears will prevent you from living your dreams.

2. Living with unquestioned assumptions about the nature of your roles will keep you needlessly constrained.

3. It's impossible to experience something new and exhilarating without stepping out of your comfort zones.

FROM MY LIFE TO YOURS

In the early years of my marriage, I assumed my role as wife was to mold myself toward the desires of my husband. If Don lived a narrow life, I was to live a narrow life. I assumed it was selfish of me to want to spend money on myself or take time away to replenish. I assumed good wives and good professionals refrained from causing conflict. As I considered visiting Jamie in Nicaragua, I assumed it was inappropriate for a woman to travel alone to a third-world country. I assumed that if I pushed forward in spite of my fears, something bad would happen. These assumptions made me my own worst enemy.

How are unquestioned assumptions about the roles you play in your life holding you back?

Each of us juggles a collection of roles: self, spouse or partner, parent, child, professional, neighbor, citizen, etc. With each role, we take on a set of responsibilities and obligations, many of which seem to conflict with each other. In a culture in which we are encouraged to take on more and more roles, obligations that come with our roles often crowd out the needs of the self. Accordingly, we feel too busy, depleted, and drained.

Much of the distress we experience regarding roles is due to unquestioned assumptions. First, we assume we must take on more roles than we can realistically manage. When we are asked to chair a committee, coordinate a bake sale, take on an extra project, or serve on a task force, we are prone to say, "Yes," without carefully assessing our energy and our priorities.

Second, we adopt definitions of our roles based on outside forces, such as our parents, bosses, and culture. We take on responsibilities—as wives, workers, and community members—without questioning whether the assumptions with which we take on those responsibilities are valid.

Third, we (especially women) assume that it's selfish and uncomely to put the role of self before the needs, or even the desires, of others. We fail to establish healthy boundaries at home and work. When we do try to make room to nurture ourselves or follow a passion, we back down if our efforts cause disharmony. Perhaps this is because we assume it's our role to keep others happy.

EXERCISE #1: I DREAM

Make an entry in your journal describing what your life would be like if there were no barriers or obstacles to pursuing your dreams. Start by writing:

My dream is to. . .

(and list 25 things that you dream about)

EXERCISE #2: ROLES AND ASSUMPTIONS

1. Make a list of the roles you play in life right now.
2. Identify the assumptions you hold about these different roles.
3. Identify which of your assumptions are holding you back from living your dreams.
4. Identify those assumptions you've accepted based on messages from others or from culture.
5. Choose which assumptions you will revise or discard based on this exercise.

EXERCISE #3: LETTER TO SELF

Write a letter from yourself as an 80-year-old woman to your present-day self. In this letter, tell your present-day self what you've learned:

1. List the fears you've overcome by age 80.
2. Describe how stepping over those fears enabled you to accomplish your dreams.
3. Tell yourself what you wish you had done but didn't.
4. Lastly, give your present-day self one piece of advice to help you become unstuck.

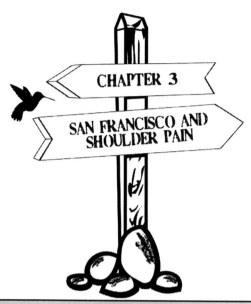

CHAPTER 3

SAN FRANCISCO AND SHOULDER PAIN

> *Courage is not the absence of fear, but rather the judgment that something else is more important than fear.*
>
> ~ Ambrose Redmoon

FIVE YEARS AFTER MY TRIP TO Nicaragua, memories of exotic experiences and the drive to repeat them continued to surface. I was forever changed. Yet, outwardly, things remained the same. Don and I had taken a few trips together, but Don's health and energy were declining. He suffered from a long-term bronchial condition. As a result, Don repeatedly contracted pneumonia, was hospitalized and treated—only to contract pneumonia again. In short, Don was old for his age while I was young for mine. When we did travel, Don set the agenda, and our trips held the emotional trappings of our everyday life.

At age 60, I celebrated my 10th year in training and organizational development at a large trucking corporation. The position provided financial security, including the benefits I needed in Don's retirement years. Yet, my corporate position gave me little pleasure or satisfaction. In fact, the whole environment felt toxic. I was restless at work and at home—ready for a new decade and yet fearful of doing something out of the normal. Why?

I had a bad case of the gremlins. According to Rick Carson, author of the classic, *Taming Your Gremlin: A Surprisingly Simple Method for Getting Out of Your Own Way*, we all have gremlins:

> A gremlin functions as an internal voice: arguing, criticizing, sucking out energy, and holding you back. A gremlin has nothing good to say and no belief in you, your dreams, or your accomplishments. If you argue with a gremlin, you get tied up in knots of anxiety, uncertainty, and misery. In short, a gremlin's whole goal is to keep you stuck.

Gremlins reside in different places for different people: in the head, the stomach, or another part of the body. Sometimes a person can visualize a gremlin; other times the gremlin is manifested in a feeling.

For me, gremlins tend to show up as voices in my head. When too many voices show up at once, I get a headache. Five years after my trip to Nicaragua, I had many headaches. The chattering voices of my gremlins were incessant. They criticized me for not acting on what I had learned when I took that trip to visit my son. At the same time, they told me to stay comfortable, not to rock the boat. According to the gremlins, I needed the security of this job, and I wasn't good for anything else anyway. Still, dreams of unique adventures kept surfacing.

During this time, I was putting together a major developmental initiative, called The Executive Leadership Institute, at the trucking company. The organizational development consultant I hired, Andrea Sigetich, introduced the company to coaching, which, at the time, was a new developmental practice in personal and business life. Immediately, I was hooked. Over a two-year period, I championed the coaching cause, worked with consultants to design the program, and became a certified professional coach.

Coaching is a one-on-one partnership between a coach and an individual, using a dialogue process to move a client forward to accomplish his or her goals. Through the process of coaching, clients deepen their knowledge, improve their performance, and enhance the quality of their lives.

Professional coaches are trained to listen and observe, customize their approach to the individual's needs, and elicit solutions and strategies from the individual. Coaches believe people are naturally creative and resourceful. The coach's role, therefore, is to bring out the strengths, capabilities, creativity, and resourcefulness of the individual in order to facilitate the achievement of the person's goals or objectives. Through the coaching process, the client gains clarity around desired objectives, gains greater awareness around choices, sets goals, and takes action.

While I was hooked on coaching, I definitely wasn't hooked on my job at the trucking company. In contrast to my chattering gremlins, which told me to stick to my safety zone, the force of the universe was sending messages telling me to stop and change the pattern of my life. Every trip I took for business resulted in a minor accident that slowed me down. I didn't see that each of these minor accidents was the universe telling me to slow down and reflect. I ignored every sign.

Meanwhile, I had become a workaholic, restless and demanding of others as well as myself. With nothing to attract my interest at home, I had taken to staying weekends on business trips so I could explore new venues. Increasingly distant from

Don, I'd lie about the need to stay the extra days. I was unconsciously running away.

One Saturday morning, after a hard workweek in San Francisco, I decided to take a walk around San Francisco Bay before heading home to another wild workweek. While walking, my mind was working a mile a minute: one gremlin was berating me about my failure to change my life. That voice was telling me it was time to change my life, slow down, and enjoy my surroundings. Another gremlin was counting all the projects I had in front of me when I returned to work, one of which I considered to be THE most important project of my career. A third gremlin was telling me that if I slowed down I'd need to reevaluate my life. The thought of doing that terrified me. It was better to leave things as they were. There was comfort in the status quo, wasn't there?

With all the voices shouting in my brain, I didn't see a crack in the sidewalk. I fell face first on the concrete and broke my shoulder. In retrospect, that crack in the sidewalk was a great metaphor for my life at the time: cracked and dangerous.

What followed was a trip to a strange hospital in San Francisco, an agonizing drug-induced experience flying across the United States, and three months of recovery, completely dependent on others for my care. Being dependent on others was agony for a woman who prides herself on being active and independent. To make matters worse, as a friend was helping me get to a doctor's appointment, I slipped and broke the shoulder a second time. I felt the universe was making sure I understood that it really was time to reevaluate my life.

By this time, my son, Jamie, was back in the States, working as a resident counselor for children with disabilities. Jamie eventually completed his Master of Science in Special Education. He dedicated his working years to teaching children with autism.

During my recovery from the accident, Jamie visited and offered the following opinion, "Mom, I believe this is the BEST thing that has ever happened to you. Maybe now you will take this recovery time to consider what is really important in your life."

Somehow, Jamie's words broke through my gremlin-induced paralysis. For the remainder of my convalescence, I reflected on my priorities and formulated a vision for my future. I decided to squarely face my fears and uncertainties; examine and validate the expectations I had about them; put together a plan to step through those fears; and step into action.

Once Jamie's words broke through my paralysis, I knew what I needed to do and how to coach myself forward. I began by designing a vision for what I absolutely wanted and what I no longer wanted in my life. I knew without reservation that working in a fast-paced, stressful corporate environment was no longer a viable choice.

As I reflected on my life, I realized my happiest days were when I was in business for myself. Years ago, I owned a bookkeeping and desktop publishing business that I ran part-time out of my home. During those years, I raised Jamie and provided support for my mother who lived in Philadelphia. When Don retired, our needs changed, and I took a full-time job.

My experiences in corporate America had expanded my skill set considerably, and once again, I wanted to be an entrepreneur. Implementing a coaching practice would allow me to live this dream.

Once I created a vision for the future, I began to uncover and test assumptions that were holding me back from fulfilling my vision. Three primary assumptions blocked my path:

1. I'm too old to start a business. What nonsense for a woman at 60+ to start a new career in a difficult economy. Maybe some other woman at 60+ can do it, but I don't have the self-confidence.

2. I can't afford the loss of financial security. With Don retired, I am our primary bread winner. How will I support us while establishing a paying clientele when I'll be starting a new business with no capital?

3. I can't build a client base without an established network. My last 10 years have been devoted entirely to corporate life. I have no network outside the corporate environment. How can I establish a new network and gain clients fast enough to succeed?

Once I found the courage to name my primary fears, I actually had fun testing the assumptions behind them.

As for my fear of being too old, I discovered through research that many women in their early 60s were starting their own businesses. Adding that information to the fact that I felt and looked like I was in my early 40s, I began to realize that "I'm too old" was not a valid assumption. It might have been a valid assumption for women of my mother's generation, but not for mine.

Testing the second assumption, "I can't afford the loss of financial security," was a bit trickier. However, I had taught others how to put together a business plan, and I knew how to market myself and put together realistic guidelines for gaining clients.

Don was supportive of my desire to begin a business, perhaps because he liked the idea of having me home with him. He offered to use an insurance policy to pay off our mortgage and install an office in the basement. With this backing, I visited my local banker and asked for a line of credit. Within minutes I was asked, "How much do you want?" One more assumption knocked down.

Another approach I used to test the security assumption was to explore the possibility of expanding my adjunct teaching at a local college. I had been teaching a course called Human Resource Management at Chatham College (now Chatham University). When I told the Director of the MBA program I was interested in teaching more, she asked, "What would it take to get you to join our department on a full-time basis?"

After some consideration, I answered, "Give me an office, a title of Assistant Professor, medical and other benefits, and your permission to continue building my coaching practice on the side." I figured, "What can I lose by asking for the world?"

Little did I know the director would say, "Yes." This win-win solution allowed me to step over my fear of becoming a bag lady.

My third assumption, that I couldn't build a business without an established network when I left corporate life, was the most difficult to overcome. I had to trust that with perseverance, persistence, and patience, the network would find me and clients would come. After all, throughout my life I had been able to adapt to my surroundings and build professional and personal relationships. At this point, I needed to trust my intuition that I was on the right path.

Once I established my vision of becoming an entrepreneur and completed the process of healing from my injuries, it was finally time to begin anew. Armed with a sense of self-worth and self-confidence, I walked into my boss' office to turn in my letter of resignation. Instead of accepting my resignation, my boss tore up the letter and told me to go back to work.

Every month for the next six months, we repeated the same scenario, until one day I presented my boss with two choices: we established a date for my leaving or I walked out the door that very day. Talk about taking a risk. However, that did the trick; he finally realized I was serious. Together, we put together an exit strategy, and six months later, I was officially retired from corporate life and moving on to new challenges and opportunities. I had done my homework and knew intuitively that I was in control of my life and resilient enough to make it work.

I started my second career at the age of 60+ as a full-time assistant professor in an MBA program, where I had the privilege of interacting with students in a nurturing environment. Thus began a three-year journey that supported my household, showed me what my passion really was (and still is), and set the stage for the rest of my life.

> *Invoke the Imagination; Provoke the Senses; Evoke the Emotions*
> ~Vision statement of the Cirque du Soleil

PRINCIPLES TO PROPEL YOU FORWARD

1. Listening to the gremlin voices in your head will sabotage you and hold you back.

2. A clearly written vision statement will define the future you want to create and serve as a rallying call to energize you into movement.

FROM MY LIFE TO YOURS

Cirque du Soleil is one of my very favorite groups; in fact, I've seen about 10 of their shows so far. If you've seen a Cirque show, you know the vision statement, quoted above, guides every performance.

My own vision began years ago when my own coach asked me to write a vision story.

I drew a picture of me living in a smallish townhome surrounded by lots of books and windows. My home had a view of the mountains. There was water nearby. My vision was of an open home, where people loved to come and gather for conversation or just to "be." I had a room where people came to crash for a night, a week, or as long as they needed as they went through their own transitions.

In my vision, my coaching practice was flourishing though the focus had changed to facilitating weekend retreats for women, especially those in transition. These workshops were based on my recently published book.

Today, I am living the vision I created for myself. Women regularly come to my home. Once here, they visibly relax; when it's time to leave, they drag their feet. You are reading the book I envisioned.

What about you? Do you have a clear vision for the rest of your life? As you think about it, here are some tips for writing your own vision statement.

EXERCISE #1: WRITE A VISION STORY

- A well-defined vision describes your future dreams and reflects who you are and who you want to become. Its sole purpose is to energize you into movement by stretching your boundaries and getting you out of your comfort zone. It can generally begin as a dream of what could be possible, if only . . . .

- Write in the first person and in the present tense.

- Begin at the end. Write your vision story beginning 10 years in the future. Write about what you are doing; the people with whom you are doing these things; how old you are and how old your companions are. Describe your surroundings and actions in detail.

- Write your vision story as if it has already happened.
- Write about how you are living out your passion.
- Once you've clarified your vision 10 years out, consider writing a vision of each year that got you to the final picture. In other words, what were you doing in year 9 that got you to year 10? What were you doing in year 8 to move toward your vision? And so on.

Have fun with this exercise. Be creative. If you are not a writer, draw a collage, or make a visual map. One of my clients did a collage of pictures to depict each year of her vision to live in France, owning a small coffee shop. She framed her collage and hung it in her kitchen to remind her of her dream. Today she lives in Paris and owns the coffee shop of her dreams.

EXERCISE #2: EXPOSE YOUR GREMLIN

1. Write a bio of your own gremlin. Describe the most common messages you hear from it. Try to identify the origin of the messages.
2. Name your gremlin.
3. Draw your gremlin.

EXERCISE #3: TEST YOUR ASSUMPTIONS

Identify three assumptions that hold you back from fulfilling your vision. Test these assumptions. Are they valid?

EXERCISE #4: STEP THROUGH YOUR FEARS

The following exercise will help you think through your fears and ultimately step through them.

Choose one risky thing you want to do but are afraid to. Write your thoughts in a journal with the following to guide you:

1. What exactly are you afraid of? For example, are you afraid of being rejected? Of being wrong? Of failing or making a mistake? Of being embarrassed or criticized?

2. What part of this fear is valid? (Your belief doesn't make a fear true.)

3. Make a list of evidence that supports your fear. Make a list of evidence that refutes it. Estimate the probability of your fear actually happening.

4. After analyzing your fear, review the truths about your fear and describe how your life will change if you step through this fear. What is the best that can happen? What is the worst that can happen? What if you do nothing?

5. Repeat with other fears.

CHAPTER 4

NO CLIENTS - NO BUSINESS - A NEW SAAB CONVERTIBLE

> *The bravest thing you can do when you are not brave is to profess courage and act accordingly.*
> ~ Cora May White Harris

D URING MY TIME AT CHATHAM, I couldn't wait to get out of bed each morning. While the ride across town to campus was hectic, life could not be better. Chatham University, founded as Chatham College for Women in 1869, has a long tradition of serving women. While the university's offerings now include co-ed programs, the commitment to serve women remains strong.

At Chatham, I learned that I LOVE teaching adult students. I LOVE challenging students with practical information they can use the moment they step out of the classroom. I LOVE the academic environment where one really is his or her own boss.

Teaching is entrepreneurial in nature. A person succeeds or fails depending on the amount of effort put forth. Even though academic red tape made my corporate experience with red tape pale by comparison, once I closed the door of the classroom, I was in charge. In the classroom, all my years of work experience came together.

While we had textbooks in my Chatham classes, I always began a class by asking questions, a core coaching approach to life and learning. For example:

- You read the chapter on marketing; now how will you apply that information in your own organization and in your own life?
- What are your experiences around marketing?
- What did you learn? How will what you learned enable you to improve your own marketing?

The students loved my approach to teaching. Now, 10 years later, students still go out of their way to let me know my classes were the best they ever had. For instance, Tina, one of my early students, recently sent me an e-mail that said, "I am grateful for the knowledge I gained earning my MBA and in particular for you . . . . I know I am able to approach my life changes with strength and in a thoughtful way because of your previous countenance. I appreciate your beautiful spirit."

I designed and taught a course on coaching, which led me to dig even deeper into how coaching works. In the process, I became more and more committed to coaching as a personal and professional developmental approach. In my interactions with students, I fine-tuned my own leadership and coaching skills as well as those of the students.

In addition to my teaching load, I established a mentoring program, pairing students with leading professional women from the business community. Where the idea of networking to establish my coaching business was intimidating, the idea of approaching women to serve students was not.

At the time, Chatham was building an advisory board of female executives—a forum for women to mentor women. I created and coordinated public workshops to attract and serve the executives, building a community and establishing Chatham as a valuable resource for women executives. What I didn't know at the time was that I was building a professional network and establishing myself as a valuable resource for women executives!

I joined the Pittsburgh Coaches Association, first serving as a board member and eventually as president. Once again, I was providing leadership, establishing credibility, and gaining visibility as well as making connections along the way. In all of this, I was playing a bigger game without realizing it. Because the effort was for the students rather than myself, it seemed easy. I was driven by a passion to serve.

Three years after I took the full-time job at Chatham, I followed my personal vision and resigned my position so I could officially build my coaching practice. I now had the network and credibility to attract clients. Closing my office door for the final time, I was full of self-confidence. I had paved the way; building the coaching practice would be easy from here. Or so I thought.

For the next six months, I spent lots of money (that I did not have) marketing my coaching and leadership development services. I made phone calls, mailed post cards, and invested in ads in *The Pittsburgh Business Times* and *Pittsburgh Post-Gazette*. I purchased an exhibit table and paid for an expensive program ad at an event featuring Mrs. Fields of Mrs. Fields' Cookies. I gained zero new clients. I watched the money trickle through my fingers, and still I persevered.

Six months is a long time for business to go badly. I continued to be rejected and dejected until, one day, disillusioned and contemplating returning to a corporate job, I drove by a Saab dealership.

Reminded that I had always wanted a Saab convertible—and not having anything else to do—I walked aimlessly into the dealership, just to look and dream about what I would be able to afford WHEN my coaching practice was successful.

By the end of the day, I had traded in my car for a bright royal blue, sexy Saab convertible that was very expensive and totally outside my financial resources. I still don't know if I was practicing "fake it until you make it" or simply acting out of disillusionment.

Oddly, once people in my network saw me driving around in that convertible, they seemed to assume I was a successful coach and called me to learn more about my services. Business began to pour in. With some combination of that Saab and my hard work, I became what people assumed I was. That was 10 years ago. With patience and perseverance, I have been successfully coaching since then, and my passion for what I do spurs me to continue, even as I am past normal retirement.

My years at Chatham represent much more than a stepping stone. Chatham was the place I discovered and embraced my vocational passion.

Before Chatham, I knew I loved learning; I knew I loved the entrepreneurial approach to life; and I knew I loved people. I didn't know that these things would combine into a passion for helping women, especially women in transition, to learn, grow, and move forward.

While I was engrossed in my work at Chatham, Don and Jamie were continuing along their own life journeys. Don developed prostate cancer and was in treatment for several years before recovering. Meanwhile, Jamie developed a deep love for Alice, a woman he believed would be his life partner. Together, Jamie and Alice invited me to join them on a travel adventure. Full of self-confidence from having successfully taken new risks, I was ready.

> *Don't be afraid of the space between your dreams and reality. If you can dream it, you can make it so.*
> ~ Belva Davis

PRINCIPLES TO PROPEL YOU FORWARD

1. It's important to pay attention to what you love, and then build that love into your life and vision.
2. The image you project to the world will help or hinder you in fulfilling your life's dreams.
3. The right relationships open a path to realizing your vision.

FROM MY LIFE TO YOURS

Working at Chatham, I didn't even know I was building relationships for my own coaching practice as well as for Chatham. I was too insecure to "put myself out there" for my own business, but I was comfortable and eager to do this for the students and the college. How is this true for you?

In general, women tend to be more comfortable and secure when they're acting in the best interests of others. It takes courage and perseverance to focus 100% attention on marketing yourself.

One of my clients, Brenda, is working hard to become an accountant. She bravely quit her full-time executive position in a large company to start her own practice. It has taken her a year of 100% networking and marketing to get the influx of clients she needs to succeed.

Brenda has given free "Lunch-n-Learn" talks in organizations and served on boards. She has built relationships by giving freely of her time and expertise. Brenda's confidence is soaring, and she is reaping the rewards of her hard work. She has built a reputation as someone people want to have on their side. Brenda is doing well because of perseverance, a willingness to invest in herself and her dream, and the productive relationships she built through networking.

The goal of networking is to develop mutually beneficial relationships. It is not, however, a linear activity. There is a monumental give and take.

To be a successful networker, you must give of yourself without expecting any direct return. You may be generous in certain relationships without ever seeing something come back. Mysteriously, however, the return will come from places unexpected.

EXERCISE #1: READER'S CHOICE

Choose three of the following actions to take within the next month:

1. Join an organization that aligns with your business interests. Regularly attend meetings. Join a committee or find a way to volunteer. These are the best ways to build mutually beneficial relationships.

2. Offer to work the registration table at an event you plan to attend. Introduce yourself in the process. You'll find it easier to talk with people at the event once you've said hello.

3. Take a leadership role in an organization to which you belong.

4. Join a charity or cause that attracts people who align with your networking needs. Join a committee or find a way to volunteer.

5. Invite someone to lunch with the intent of learning about his or her goals. Ask this question, "As a person in

your network, what can I do for you?" Repeat this step each month.

6. Send a congratulatory note to someone who has recently been recognized.

7. Send a thank-you note to someone who gives freely to an organization to which you belong.

8. Build or revise a LinkedIn profile (www.LinkedIn.com). Make sure you list your accomplishments. While you might be hesitant to toot your own horn, this is essential to building your credibility.

9. Find three people you know on LinkedIn and add a sincere recommendation to their profile. Chances are they will return the favor.

10. Devote two hours to looking at your contacts on LinkedIn. Discover shared and potential contacts. Ask your contacts to introduce you electronically or by phone. Repeat once per quarter.

11. Join a LinkedIn group, based on your interests and goals. Get involved. Pose a question. Participate in group conversations.

EXERCISE #2: IMAGE: FAKE IT UNTIL YOU MAKE IT

There are many psychological reasons to fake self-confidence when you are not feeling it. Practicing a few simple strategies can make the difference between someone taking you seriously or not. Remember the saying, "If you think you will fail, you will"? The opposite is also true, "If you think you will succeed, you will."

Inner confidence is a learned skill. With practice and a few simple strategies, you can positively influence how people view you. I bought a car that I couldn't afford and drove it proudly. I also dressed as though I were on the top of the world. Only I knew some of my accessories were more than 10 years old.

I'm not suggesting you act irresponsibly or go into debt to look successful. I am suggesting you hold your head high and project yourself as a winner. Here are some things you might try:

1. Take the initiative to introduce yourself to three people you don't know at a networking event. Smile and ask each person a "get to know you" question.

2. Send an article, link, or other resource to someone you admire professionally. Make this a regular practice.

3. Take the initiative to welcome visitors to your professional organization. This is not only gracious; it makes you look like a leader.

4. To the best of your ability, dress the part of the professional you want to be. While it doesn't make sense to overspend, it often does make sense to make a few strategic investments.

5. Publish a regular newsletter or blog even if you feel you are still figuring things out. Ask people you admire to be guest contributors.

6. Pay careful attention to your body language. Walk with your head held high, make eye contact, smile, and offer a firm handshake.

7. Avoid apologizing unless you have a good reason.

EXERCISE #3: WHAT CHANGE?

What change have you been longing to make but the rational side of you keeps putting it off? For example, buying a pair of diamond earrings, renting a house by the beach, etc.

CHAPTER 5

MACHU PICCHU, RUBBER LEGS, AND MANTRAS

> *If you play it safe in life, you've decided that you don't want to grow anymore.*
>
> ~ Shirley Hufstedler

IN 2003, DURING MY TIME AT CHATHAM, Jamie and Alice, the woman he believed would be his life partner, decided to spend a month exploring Peru. They invited me to join them at the end of their trip to take a four-day trek over the Inca Trail to the Machu Picchu ruins.

At the time of this invitation, I was 62, thrilled to be learning I had a talent and passion for teaching, and that I was in fact an excellent instructor. I was also learning that years in a corporate environment and my skills as a professional coach were perfectly aligned with my role as faculty member. I was constantly learning new skills, learning to take risks in my life, and learning to accept challenges that a few years before I would not have dared to try. When Jamie and Alice invited me on this adventure, I was ready—or so I thought.

Machu Picchu is a pre-Columbian Inca ruin located at an elevation of approximately 7,710 feet. To reach the ruin, you climb several mountain passes situated at 14,000 to 15,000 feet above sea level. Then you climb down a series of steep steps to the ruin, in the middle of a beautiful nowhere.

When Alice broke up with Jamie, leaving him shocked and deeply hurt, our plans were disrupted. Then Don's doctor scheduled surgery and radiation treatments to address his prostate cancer, to begin the day before we were scheduled to leave.

"Mom," Jamie said, "You need to go and climb your own mountain. I'll stay home and take care of Dad."

Ann, an adventuresome divorced mother of two, who happened to be a good friend and world traveler, agreed to accompany me. Athletic and in her early 50s, Ann was ready for the challenge. Off we went.

The Machu Picchu trip was such a turning point in my life, that some details from Chapter 1 bear repeating.

I spent most of the first day on the Inca Trail trying to figure out how to stop hiking and get back down the mountain the easiest and fastest way possible. I could then take the bus and meet the group at the Sun Gate, the entrance to the Machu Picchu ruins, on the fourth day. I was enjoying nothing about the hike. Putting one foot in front of the other in the climb was the most difficult thing I'd ever done.

In spite of the guides, Shay and Mario, pushing me to eat and drink, I couldn't do either. I struggled to breathe and was convinced I could go no farther.

Sweating and struggling, I berated myself for having illusions, believing I could climb nearly 15,000 feet at age 62. I felt the weight of my years and the loss of the opportunities that come with youth. I wanted nothing more than to climb back down the mountain and feel sorry for myself. Unfortunately, there was no easy path down that mountain.

That first night, exhausted, I decided that my mental perspective was holding me back. I promised myself on the following day, when we climbed the highest point over Dead Woman's Pass, I was going to think positively and focus on making it to camp that evening.

When altitude sickness struck the second day, a defeated mantra reverberated in my brain, "I got to get off this mountain. I got to get off this mountain." With each reverberation, I became more and more scared.

I took sips of water, trying to follow the advice of the guides. I could not urinate and I couldn't eat.

As we crossed Dead Woman's Pass, the highest point, the mantra changed its refrain, "Not going to make it. Not going to make it." I began to weave. I could no longer drink. I upchucked. The guides gave me oxygen and cocaine leaves (a stimulant) to chew.

"I'm not going to make it. I'm not going to make it."

I know that Shay and Mario positioned themselves, one on each side of me, to keep me going. Yet, I have no memory of coming over the pass, the most beautiful part of the hike. I laid in a stupor all night, missing the camp surroundings entirely.

On the third day, I woke up weary but determined. I deliberately changed my mantra to, "I can do this. I can do this."

It was on that day that Shay, Mario, and I somehow got out of the protocol for safety and I fell, head first, over the side of the mountain. Shay and Mario pulled me out by my feet, and I lost my glasses in the process.

We still had eight hours left of descending steps so steep they seemed nearly vertical to me. I adjusted the mantra in my head, "I can do this. One step and drop. I can do this. One step and drop." I made it to camp on legs that felt like rubber.

I don't know how, on the following day, I woke at 3:30 a.m. feeling like a million bucks. I pulled on my hiking boots, and kept up with the group as we hiked to the Sun Gate. Granted, I had to crawl part of the way, but I made it! The feeling was amazing—I had pushed myself beyond what I thought was my limit, and I made it! The mantra in my head that day, "I made it. I made it. I can't believe I made it!"

I returned home from Machu Picchu with the confidence to accomplish anything I set out to do, more confidence than I had had the first 62 years of my life. I had battled a mountain and won.

With the confidence came a sense of calm and strength, physically and mentally. Little could cause me stress after my trip. I felt strong—powerful—ready to tackle the world.

At the time of the Machu Picchu trip, I had relationships with students, a growing network of women, and a small number of coaching clients. As the women at Chatham heard the stories of my hike, I became a freshly minted role model for younger women: "If Donna can climb a mountain at age 62, I can find the courage to make the changes I desire. If Donna can find the strength and courage to step back from an emotionally battered marriage to fulfill a dream, I can find courage to navigate destructive situations, too."

I suddenly possessed a new sense of credibility as well as confidence. I knew about transition, change, fear, and courage. I knew about taking risks. I could confidently walk the talk of helping people move through their own transitions and emerge at the other end, successful and confident about where they are heading.

With the new me, my relationship with Don had to change. The new me that had begun to break free in Nicaragua would never be imprisoned by needs for security or pleasing others again. I knew there were more mountains to climb, all over the world, more exotic ruins, and natural sights unseen. I felt compelled to see them all. I felt compelled to hike them all.

Yet, I was married to Don. I had made the decision to stay in the marriage. Both compassion and integrity compelled me to honor Don and my commitment to him in daily ways.

Don survived his medical treatment while I was away. In fact, Don would eventually completely recover from cancer, but not for a few years. In general, however, Don's general health was declining, and my caregiving role was increasing. At the same time, I felt young again, with a strong desire to pursue things I had missed in my youth. I was bent on climbing mountains, even in the context of my marriage to an ailing 81-year-old man.

As for my son, Jamie managed his own heartbreak while I was away. Healing was a long way off, and Jamie still needed my support. My mother's heart considered Jamie a key priority in my life, especially since Don was so critical of him.

How to balance the needs of my family with the person I was becoming? The push and pull of this would be with me for a very long time.

> *Think left and think right and think low and think high. Oh, the thinks you can think up if only you try!*
> ~ Dr. Seuss

PRINCIPLES TO PROPEL YOU FORWARD

1. The choices you make when confronted with tough situations propel you forward or set you back.

2. Every time you make a positive choice, you turn yourself into someone a little stronger.

3. Controlling your self-talk (internal dialogue) is essential to controlling your life and realizing your vision.

4. Your thoughts and beliefs (enabling beliefs or limiting beliefs) propel you forward or hold you back.

FROM MY LIFE TO YOURS

During my journey on the mountain, my initial mantra (self-talk) was, "I can't do this! I can't do this!" If I had continued to think that way, I would have been unable to complete the climb. I would have failed to climb the mountain. That would have been a significant life-altering failure.

My initial mantra qualified as a limiting belief that was controlling my behavior on the mountain. I believed I could not make it any farther, and I was struggling with all my might. When I changed my mantra to, "I can do this. One step and drop," my behavior also changed. As you know, the outcome also changed.

While the new mantra didn't make it any easier to climb the mountain, it helped me make it to the Machu Picchu ruins with the rest of the group. This trip completely altered my perspective on what I was able to accomplish. When I completed this trip, I knew I could do anything I put my mind to.

Let's think about mountains. To climb a mountain, you toil, you sweat, and you finally reach the top. Then what do you get? According to Mark Sanders and Tia Sillers, authors of *I Hope You Dance Journal,* you get a sense of accomplishment, peace, and a sense of satisfaction from doing what you set out to do— and you get a great view of the next mountain. That next mountain is looming, challenging, and calling your name.

On the other hand, once you've climbed a mountain, the next one doesn't look quite so scary. Each mountain I've climbed over the years has been real. Each involved overcoming the fear that I wouldn't be able to complete the climb; each involved toil and sweat; and yes, finally, each resulted in an exhilarating feeling that I'd done the very best I could and in most cases reached the top.

Climbing mountains is also a metaphor for life challenges. From each mountain I physically climbed, I found a lesson that helps me also climb and conquer my metaphorical mountains, the challenges that come with life and the fears I face in realizing my vision.

This mountain metaphor takes me out of my head and allows my heart to feel empowered. I realize that although life requires arduous climbs, I can make it to the top every time. I can face my fears and overcome them.

EXERCISE #1: PUSH AND PULL

1. Describe the push and pull in your life.
2. Describe how you typically respond to the tension.
3. In what ways do you sacrifice yourself?
4. In what ways do you keep moving forward?
5. What other choices could you make?

EXERCISE #2: LIMITING AND ENABLING BELIEFS

1. Identify one choice you are afraid to make because of limiting beliefs.
2. Identify the ways in which you behave in alignment with those beliefs. In other words, what do people see you doing or saying because of your limiting beliefs? Be honest with yourself.
3. Identify the results you could achieve if you made the choice you are afraid to make.

4. Identify new behaviors you need to exhibit to get to those results.

5. Identify enabling beliefs that will help you to change to the new behaviors.

CHAPTER 6

ROLE MODELS, THE ISLE OF IONA, AND MCMASTERS SCOTCH WHISKEY

> *Learn to get in touch with the silence within yourself and know that everything in this life has a purpose.*
> ~ Elisabeth Kubler Ross

A T THE SAME TIME I WAS TEACHING AT CHATHAM and building my coaching practice, I became an affiliate of The Center for Leadership Studies (CLS) in Escondido, California. In this capacity, as a Master Certified Trainer of Trainers, I gained entrance to some lucrative organizational leadership projects as well as built a worldwide connection to other CLS affiliates.

Marshall Goldsmith, a coach who got his start at CLS, is now the world's most recognizable coach and author of numerous leadership and coaching books.

Goldsmith and his partner, Howard Morgan, presented a training program to certify representatives of the Center's worldwide affiliates in their behavioral coaching process. Of the 15 people invited to participate, only 2 of us were professionally trained coaches. We felt confident of ourselves as we listened to Goldsmith and Morgan teaching the rest of the group basic coaching skills.

My own cockiness, however, was short lived. During the week of training, Goldsmith and Morgan each approached me separately with feedback. Both gave fundamentally the same message, "Donna, you do a wonderful job of explaining and teaching. What we see, though, is that you are continually playing small in this group. Instead of teaching about coaching, BE a coach and role model for the others. Let's see you play a bigger game."

After I picked myself up off the floor, got over my embarrassment that someone had seen through me, and thought about what playing large really meant, I began to practice playing large. I took risks, honestly shared my opinions, and trusted my intuition. What a difference the change in perspective made in the dynamics for the rest of that week and beyond! I made a commitment to myself never to play small again. Although my resolve has been tested repeatedly, it's never been broken. Marshall and Howard's advice plays in my mind every time I feel myself playing small, reverting to security-based behaviors.

Another influence in my quest to live large was (and is) a woman named Joan Anderson. A few years before my encounter with Goldsmith and Morgan, I had read Joan's first book, *A Year by the Sea: Thoughts of an Unfinished Woman*. The book tells the story of Joan's marriage, how she left her husband and lived one year alone in a small cottage by the sea. Joan's story resonated with me. Her story described what I wanted but was too afraid to do. I was certainly an unfinished woman.

Included at the end of Joan's *A Year by the Sea* is a website and description of "Weekends by the Sea" retreats Joan holds for women who see themselves as unfinished and want to renew their lives. My intuition told me I needed to attend one of Joan's retreats. Without hesitation, I made a call and soon headed to Cape Cod.

The following description from Joan's website describes the process women go through at one of her retreats:

> The hallmark of these retreats is utilizing nature— finding metaphors for our lives from that which is presented during a contemplative hike on a great barrier beach. The three days are as predictable as the tides and as spontaneous as the changeable weather. The participants work with their intuition and instincts—strengths which have become thread-bare because modern women lead such hectic lives and play so many different roles. Most women leave after three days rejuvenated and with new intentions firmly intact—determined to re-arrange their lives in their own images.

My retreat by the sea with Joan was one of the important steps in my quest to live life on my own terms. Joan's message was in complete harmony with the advice I received from Gold-smith and Morgan. After the retreat, I read all of Joan's books and continued to find her materials deeply inspiring.

A few years later, I sensed I should take a deeper plunge and sign up for a spiritual retreat with Joan on the Isle of Iona, off the west coast of Scotland. The timing conflicted with an-other opportunity to take a unique adventure, and I had a hard choice to make. I had an internal sense, an intuition, that I needed to take the trip to Iona, disappointing as it would be to miss the other opportunity.

I thought I might have misunderstood my intuition, how-ever, when the trip was full, and I was put on a waiting list. Two days later, Joan's assistant called to say there was a cancellation. Did I still want to go? Without hesitation, I said, "Yes!"

As a past center of Irish monasticism, the Isle of Iona has a strong spiritual history. The island culture is filled with stories of buried Scottish kings, reincarnation, channeling, and other occurrences. People go to Iona for tranquility, natural beauty, and spiritual retreats.

In the days before the trip, anticipating the winter cold on the coastal island, I visited a specialty sock shop in a local mall to buy hiking socks. The owner, whose name I learned was Nina, asked where I was heading. When I explained that I was going to one of Joan Anderson's retreats, Nina began to cry, saying, "You'll not believe this." Nina walked into her back office and brought out one of Joan's books, explaining that she had just finished the book the night before. This conversation between two strangers was the beginning of an eight-year friendship—as well as a confirmation that I should indeed be going on this trip.

As I prepared for another life-changing trip, however, I had no idea that even getting to the retreat would test my mettle. I had developed a habit of packing for trips at the last minute because I was fearful a change in Don's health would require me to cancel at the last minute. I didn't want to get excited about a trip only to have to cancel.

On the day of travel to Iona, expecting to leave the house in the afternoon, I began to pack at 10 a.m. Thirty minutes later, I received a call from the airline. Because of Hurricane Wilma, all flights out of Pittsburgh after 12:30 p.m. were being canceled. If I could get to the airport by noon, the airline would book me on the last flight out. In some distress, I threw things into a suitcase and rushed out the door. I made the flight with exactly two minutes to spare—an inauspicious beginning for my first trip to Europe alone.

During my layover at Kennedy International Airport, I had five hours to get organized and worry about what I had neglected to pack. Feeling disoriented, I was rethinking my decision to go on this trip. In general, I was feeling miserable. I had been so proud of myself for taking another plunge into playing large, and look what had happened.

Don and I had fought about this trip in a way that would become a pattern. He protested loudly at first. I held my ground. Eventually, Don gave in to my decision but continued to protest in subtle ways. In my discombobulated state at the airport, I was wondering if Don was correct. Maybe world traveling wasn't for me. Maybe I should just stay at home and live small. Lots of gremlins and head chatter were racing in my brain.

With plenty of time until my departure, I decided to visit my gate. Perhaps I could spot other women who were going on the same trip. Perhaps these women were feeling as small as I was. By the time we boarded that plane to Glasgow, I had bonded with 5 of the 18 women who would be on the retreat.

Then the endurance test of getting to Iona began. The trip from Pittsburgh to Iona took 48 hours, and I didn't sleep. We took a flight from Kennedy to Glasgow and then rode a train for roughly seven hours to the village of Oban, where we spent the night. We held our own in pouring rain and blasting wind as we boarded a ferry to the small Isle of Mull. In a raging storm, we rode a bus from Craignure, at one end of the island, to Fionnphort, at the other end, to board a ferry to Iona. Because the weather had delayed our arrival, we had to run with our luggage for nearly a mile to catch the final ferry of the day.

Iona, roughly 10 miles long and 1 mile wide, is bordered on the west by the Atlantic Ocean and the east by the Sound of Iona. During our entire stay, the weather was stormy and eerily tempestuous, with raging winds and bone-chilling rain. We were on a coastal island during the winter solstice, experiencing the aftermath of a hurricane. Those warm socks I bought got a lot of use.

The content of the retreat resembled my earlier retreat with Joan, with more depth. The setting of Iona and the timing of the retreat contributed to a deep spiritual sense. Each morning, we met with Joan and with Delores Whelan, a Celtic philosopher. In the afternoons, we had time to reflect on our own, and then time to roam the island. We were instructed to observe silence in order to listen internally as well as gain the most benefit from this remote and spiritual island.

We were also instructed to carry the following questions with us throughout the retreat:

- What is the metaphor for your quest for clarity in your life?
- How does your intuition guide your life?
- How do you tap into your intuition on a regular basis?

As I wandered Iona, I learned to deeply listen and watch what happens when I am in solitude. As I wandered, gulls seemed to cross my path continually. On one of my solo walks, I wrote a poem about my experience with the sea gulls. From that poem came the metaphor for my life at that time, "Spread my wings. Do not turn back right now! The timing is perfect." From that point, my questions became, "Where will I soar? When will I soar? How will I know it's time?"

On some days, my intuition urged me to ignore the instruction to roam alone in silence. On those days, I paired up with Frankie, a woman in her late 70s who was suffering and recuperating from a debilitating near-death experience with a nerve illness. Frankie and I talked about life, love, and our disappointments. Mostly, we simply laughed aloud.

Invariably Frankie and I ended up in a little Scottish pub, having hot tea with several shots of McMasters Scotch Whiskey. Sometimes we just had the whiskey. Dang it; we were cold. After all, we were on a coastal island; the weather was rainy, damp, cold, hurricane-aftermath kind of weather. Did I say we were COLD?

Frankie and I talked with old-timers in the pub, having a great time learning about the culture and the people of the island. I learned the most, however, from Frankie herself, as she was the first older woman whose vitality in the midst of difficult circumstances served as a role model.

Frankie, who had experienced deep losses, lived in chronic pain. Yet, joy rather than sadness radiated from Frankie, and her life seemed anything but over. She provided a glimpse into the difference a perspective can make, and I began to believe I could learn new things and do anything I wanted to do, no matter how old I happened to be. Frankie's example was a profound gift. I left her presence believing that age is not a constrictor. Rather, age is enlightening and the pathway to ever increasing new experiences. Frankie's example was among the most inspiring elements of the Iona retreat.

As I left the island, I had little idea how much the experience of Joan's teaching, Frankie's example, and my self-reflection would influence the rest of my life. The determination to live large and keep growing, no matter what life or age threw my way, had taken deep root in my very being.

> *The unexamined life is a wasted life.*
> ~ St. Augustine

PRINCIPLES TO PROPEL YOU FORWARD

1. As you learn to trust your intuition, the world around you expands exponentially.

2. Learning to play large is a gradual process that requires embracing your physical and emotional strengths.

3. Seeking role models and mentors is a worthy pursuit, as they can help you see the difference between *what is* and *what is possible.*

FROM MY LIFE TO YOURS

Again, I had a choice to make. Attending a spiritual retreat on the Isle of Iona with my mentor and role model, Joan Anderson, meant I had to miss an opportunity to take a different enticing trip occurring at the same time.

I followed my intuition to travel to Iona, and this turned out to be an important positive juncture in my life. The experience confirmed my need to trust my intuition. The solitude and interaction with Frankie and other like-minded women showed me how far I'd come in taking control over my own life.

Intuition is awareness below the surface. Following your intuition is about paying attention to your "gut" feeling and bringing it forth into your conversations and everyday life. Intuition is the gathering of non-empirical information, knowledge that cannot be verified by facts. It is non-observable.

Your intuition may express itself as a sensation, a feeling you can't shake, a visual image, a smell, a taste, or a sudden emotion or shift of energy. You might think of intuition as hunches, serendipity, guesses, divine inspiration, following your instincts, or a sixth sense.

Intuition is not about being correct in a logical way; it's about trusting your inner guidance. This isn't the same as being impulsive or imposing your values on others. Intuition serves us best when we validate it with reflection. When our intuitions are about someone else, it's important to check for validity with the other person.

In urging me to travel to Iona, my intuition was guiding me to learn intentionally from my role model, Joan, as well as to discover a new role model in Frankie. It also guided me to a concentrated time of solitude and reflection.

In our society of over-connectedness, solitude seems to be a lost art. However, solitude is necessary to accomplish our dreams and visions. Everyone needs to step back on a regular basis to reap the benefits of time alone.

Solitude invites you to just "be" silent, unwind, and find peace in your body so you are better able to handle the chaos of your life when you return. It creates the space for appreciation of the positives in your life; it helps you find peace and let go of the negatives. Solitude creates an opportunity for your intuition to rise to the surface and show you what you haven't been seeing or hearing.

EXERCISE #1: IDENTIFY YOUR ROLE MODELS

Write about the people who have been role models in your life and describe how each has contributed. Then think about the people in your life, professionally and personally, that you admire. What qualities are these individuals modeling that you might emulate?

EXERCISE #2: EXPLORE YOUR INTUITION

Explore how your intuition speaks to you. Make a list of the words and phrases you use to describe the world around you. Think about the words you use in conversations with others. Notice your own sense preferences.

Do you use visual phrases, such as the following?

- I see
- It's crystal clear

Are you more likely to use auditory phrases, such as these?

- I hear you
- It sounds like a good idea

Are you more likely to use kinesthetic phrases, such as the following?

- Let's bounce some ideas around
- I feel good about the decision

What sense-oriented phrases do you use on a regular basis? Are you predominantly visual, auditory, or kinesthetic? Your sense preferences help you to identify messages from your intuition.

EXERCISE #3: PAY ATTENTION TO YOUR INTUITION

When you have identified your predominant sense preferences, take some time to be alone—a minimum of 20 minutes. Embrace solitude and pay attention to your intuition.

For example, if you are an auditory person, listen to the music of the world. You might try taking a walk and listening to the sound of birds, water, trees, frogs, and insects. You might sit quietly in a room with the lights turned low. Listen to your mind as you consciously think about your daydreams, inhibitions, and wishes.

If you are a visual person, you might try a walk through an art museum. If you are a kinesthetic person, you might try a brisk run.

In any case, follow your sense preference and then describe what your intuition is telling you.

A CELTIC BLESSING

DEEP PEACE
of the running wave to you

DEEP PEACE
of the flowing air to you

DEEP PEACE
of the shining stars to you

DEEP PEACE
of the son of peace

TO YOU

CHAPTER 7

CRATER LAKE NATIONAL PARK AND WILD WOMEN OF THE WEST

> *A friend may well be reckoned the masterpiece of nature.*
>
> ~ Ralph Waldo Emerson

T HE 18 WOMEN ON THE IONA RETREAT LEARNED a great deal about ourselves and a great deal about each other. One of the women insisted that Jamie and I must take a trip to Oregon. From what she had learned about Jamie and me, she felt certain we would both find peace and contentment and, more importantly, roots in Oregon. Jamie took this information to heart, did lots of research, and decided he wanted to move to Oregon. Oh, the spontaneity of the young!

Meanwhile, Don was still battling cancer and in general making life difficult for all of us. I began to try to persuade Don to sell our house and move into smaller, one-level living. Again, I took the initiative to put our townhome on the market and look for a place where Don could have his own one-level space. More importantly, I was looking for a place where I could further separate our lives, a place where I could have my own living and working space and still be available to Don. It took a number of years before the move actually took place, but the process began shortly after the trip to Iona. In the meantime, my strengths of patience and persistence were sorely tested.

Around the same time as the Iona trip, my dear friend and former consultant at the trucking corporation, Andrea Sigetich, and I were exploring the idea of starting a group of like-minded women who had a common interest in hiking beautiful places, laughing, and ingesting good food and wine. We'd call the group Wild Women and would meet on an annual basis at a different national park, staying in the lodges and hiking each day.

Andrea and I anticipated that at some point in our collective lives we would have outlived our spouses or significant others. We envisioned ourselves hiking our way into retirement and old folks' homes, happy we had bonded and experienced life apart from the men in our lives.

As it so happened, Andrea was living in Bend, Oregon, during the time we were having these discussions. Andrea took the lead to coordinate the first trip to Crater Lake, Oregon. At the same time, Jamie was planning a trip to Seattle to attend the wedding of one of his Peace Corps friends. The universe works in mysterious ways, doesn't it?

Little by little, the pieces fell into place. Jamie would fly to Seattle for the wedding and spend a week hiking by himself in Oregon. I would join him in Portland for a mother/son four-day hike before meeting up with the Wild Women for the first time.

When I met Jamie in Portland, I realized this was the first 24/7 time we would spend together since I traveled to Nicaragua to visit him five years earlier. We had both come through life-changing experiences. I wondered what it was going to be like to travel with my adult son. I'm sure he was wondering the same thing.

Throughout the four days we traveled together before meeting the Wild Women, and again when Jamie picked me up for our return flight to Pittsburgh, I was amazed at the maturity of my son. I also noticed how comfortable Jamie was in his skin. In Portland, he exuded a sense of calm, confidence, and power I hadn't seen in him in Pennsylvania. Perhaps Jamie really did need to move to this western part of the country.

While Jamie and I were hiking on one of Oregon's trails, I got a panicky cell phone call from Don. He was coughing up blood and wanted us to come home immediately. What to do?

I called Don's doctor, who said the bleeding was to be expected as part of Don's respiratory illness. He suggested Jamie and I both continue our trip and replenish ourselves. The blood marked the next phase of that particular illness. The doctor recommended we avoid stopping our lives because of it.

Jamie and I agreed to continue the trip. We made sure the doctor would call us with any major problems so we could reevaluate our decision.

This decision was one major turning point that would influence my life for the stressful years yet to come. I would accept the need to replenish myself regularly during Don's long illness.

For the moment, however, Jamie and I both needed to overcome the deep guilt that was plaguing us. We did this by continuing our hiking and talking. The push and pull was painful for both of us.

We decided to put our guilt aside for the remainder of the trip and enjoy the time we had. Mostly, we enjoyed each other's company. As we traveled together, our mother/son relationship slowly morphed into a healthy, mother/adult son/friends relationship.

When we hiked, Jamie, being the stronger hiker, went off at his pace, and I happily lagged behind at my own leisurely speed. Jamie gave me mini safety lessons on what to look for when hiking. By the end of our four days, I was confident in my ability to hike alone. It felt good—I was no longer dependent on someone else's willingness to accompany me on a hike.

Jamie and I arrived at Crater Lake one day before the Wild Women. This gave us a last evening to explore Crater Lake, have a leisurely dinner, and enjoy a brief hike. The next morning Jamie took off on his own for several days while I waited for the Wild Women to arrive.

One by one, they arrived, these women who came from executive positions in hospital administration, Fortune 100 companies, human resources, and nonprofits. All were married to equally well-established men. All had been or were currently hiking on a regular basis, including at high altitudes. Their ages ranged from 45 to 55 years old. I was the oldest by 10 or more years.

Upon arrival, none of us knew this would be the first of seven (and counting) Wild Women trips. None of us knew how important we would become to each other.

I've already shared information about Andrea, who brought all of us together. She chose the first national park and organized the hikes. If there is a Wild Women leader, Andrea is the one to recognize. Her background is in human relations and training/organizational development. Andrea recruited this group of women who, with me as the exception, all came from the western part of the United States.

Our group was comprised of a number of distinct personalities, many of whom became regulars for the annual Wild Women trips.

Meeting Linda that first time, and every time thereafter, was like reconnecting with a soul sister. We hit it off immediately and have always begun each conversation as if we shared a long history and had only been apart for a few minutes.

Like me, Linda is an executive coach. Unlike me, she lives in a house high on a hilltop in San Francisco. (I live in the suburbs of Pittsburgh.) Linda is a deep thinker who craves time alone for reflection. She became a Wild Women regular for the time alone as well as for the connection to and companionship with other women.

For Marion, on the other hand, the Wild Women trips offered refreshment from a life of caring for a mentally challenged child. On that first trip, Marion embraced the way we accepted each other as we were, without question. Over the years, I admired how Marion reinvented herself professionally from a nurse to an executive coach in a health-related nonprofit.

A financial planner, Jan is proud of the fact that she competes—and wins—in a male-dominated profession. Jan came on the Wild Women trip for the peace it offered, away from the stress of her hectic world. Jan shared her longing to travel across the Canadian Rockies in her camping truck with her two dogs. In the meantime, she was (and is) a supportive mom who watches her two daughters "find themselves."

Charlene became the Wild Women's role model for authenticity. Always living in the moment, Charlene says she didn't question life until she listened to the members of the group talking. Charlene loves the deep conversations and powerful questions that characterize Wild Women time together. Charlene's life has been enriched with the love she pours into her extended family of children, grandchildren, and great grandchildren.

As a former hospital administrator-turned-consultant and world traveler, Lois was attracted to each Wild Women trip by the adventure and deep relaxation it offered.

The person who came for the fun and adventure of the climb was Carol. She and Marion were usually the first on the mountain trails, took the longest and hardest hikes, and left the rest of us behind.

Although not on that first trip, Ann and Nina would join us on one trip or another. Ann, my Machu Picchu companion, was a wonderful addition to three Wild Women trips during her single years. Now remarried, she spends much of her time traveling the world with her husband and visiting a new granddaughter in Paris.

Nina, from whom I bought my hiking socks for the retreat on Iona, joined us for one Wild Women trip. She blended beautifully with the group, adding much laughter and fun.

Looking back, I love these women and can hardly believe how each has enriched my life. However, when I encountered the group for the first time at Crater Lake, a question kept repeating in my mind, "How on earth, at my age, am I going to keep up with these women?" I thought I must be crazy to think I could be a real hiker.

In the first Wild Women group meeting, we set a pattern for our days together. Thankfully, that pattern made it possible for me to participate fully in the group.

Each morning on that first trip, we met for coffee and a healthy breakfast. While we ate, Andrea shared her research, and we decided which hikes to tackle. The first day we explored Crater Lake in its entirety by car and stopped at overlooks for pictures. That same day we took short hikes to acclimate to the altitude. On each additional day, we chose one or two hikes, one less strenuous so individuals had a choice.

At 5 p.m. each day after a Wild Women hike, we met for hors d'oeuvres, wine, and conversation. Each woman had the opportunity to share what she had encountered throughout the day, what she had learned, and how the day had affected her life. The coach in me came forward to facilitate many of these conversations.

On the hikes and over wine, the Wild Women got to know each other, telling stories about our past, our present, and our hopes for the future. I couldn't believe the depth of the bonds we formed even on our first trip. I found a support system that would replenish and sustain me for years to come.

At the time of this writing, the Wild Women still meet each year at a national park. We follow the same pattern for each trip, with two women being host; one or two women organizing the hikes; and one or two women organizing the logistics. One of my roles on these hikes continues to be asking the coaching questions that lead to in-depth conversation.

As for my experience with the hikes at Crater Lake, there was no comparison to the experience at Machu Picchu. On the Machu Picchu trip, I had persevered and conquered the nearly 15,000 feet trek to reach the ruins. During the Crater Lake trip, I had to turn back from elevated heights of 7,000 and 8,000 feet.

My disappointment at turning back morphed into determination to become healthy and strong enough to keep up with the youngest and strongest of the group. This became a yearly goal and struggle, a quest I was determined to complete. I didn't know it at the time, but my perseverance in the face of an aging body would become a model for the younger women to emulate, just as Frankie had become a model for me on the Isle of Iona.

The first Wild Women trip to Crater Lake tested my resolve to live my life on my own terms. I learned that I could travel and explore the world while still maintaining a commitment to my husband.

When I returned home, Don's bleeding had stopped; he had survived just fine on his own. We had an enjoyable time as I shared my pictures and told stories about the trip.

During this first Wild Women trip, at age 64, I established two patterns/commitments. First, I decided to share my travels with Don so he did not feel left out. While Don couldn't participate in my travels, I realized I could still share this part of my life with him via pictures and conversation. Second, I made a commitment to set goals for each trip, goals that would allow me to build my stamina and strength to hike with the hardiest of the Wild Women. Both decisions proved to be quite a challenge in the coming years.

> *Friends are those rare people who ask how we are and then wait to hear the answer.*
>
> ~ Ed Cunningham

PRINCIPLES TO PROPEL YOU FORWARD

1. When you push yourself to live your dreams, even when it is a struggle, surprising things can happen.

2. Living large involves interacting with others who share your values, accept you for who you are, and act as a supportive community.

3. Commitment to your life vision is much easier when you make room for regular contact with a supportive network.

FROM MY LIFE TO YOURS

The initial Wild Women trip marked the first time in my life I connected deeply with a group of women. Before this, my main connections were with men, brotherly colleagues, etc. I hadn't realized the power a group of supportive women can have.

I had pushed myself to realize my dream of hiking in a national park, and I received an unexpected gift of friendship. This gift would sustain me in the years to come as my caregiving role became more intense and stressful. From the time of the first Wild Women trip, I began to prioritize making and nurturing friendships with women.

Scientists are studying the rewards of female friendship— with amazing results. Not only do friendships between women define who we are, soothe us during troubled times, and fill in the emotional gaps in our marriages; they also counteract the emotional and physical effects of stress.

For example, in a landmark study at UCLA, described in *Psychological Review* in 2000, scientists report that when women experience stress, their bodies produce a myriad of chemicals, including oxytocin. This chemical causes them to make and nurture friendships, which in turn produces more oxytocin. Oxytocin is also known as the "bonding" hormone. Women produce it in abundance when they spend time with their babies, particularly during breastfeeding. The result of a surge of oxytocin is a feeling of well-being and an urge to nurture children and befriend other women.

Harvard Medical School's famous Nurses' Health Study, which began in 1976 and provides information on 238,000 dedicated nurse-participants, found that the more friends a woman has, the more likely she is to live a long healthy life. The results were so great, scientists reason that having no friends is as dangerous to a woman's health as being overweight or smoking.

If you're like many women, the first thing you neglect when life gets busy is relationships with your female friends. This is partly because you know they'll understand and be there when you need them, no questions asked. But this is a self-defeating practice, since it is your women friends who give you the strength to meet life's challenges with insight, love, and most importantly, laughter.

On the other hand, men's friendships with other men take on a different character. For instance, men rarely come together to share their deepest feelings, especially when in a group.

When women gather, they discuss the "being" or the feelings of things. The conversation of male friends in a group deals with "doing" things and tends to be interspersed with action-packed activities, like hiking, rafting, kayaking, playing football, etc.

EXERCISE #1: UNEXPECTED GIFTS

Reflect on the times you have pushed yourself to achieve a dream, even though it was difficult. What unexpected gifts did you receive in the process?

EXERCISE #2: ASSESS YOUR FRIENDSHIPS

Make a list of the relationships you rely on for support. Women commonly accumulate relationships based on life's circumstances rather than deliberate intention. Sometimes these relationships fall short of supporting the person's dreams and vision. Some of these relationships (including relatives) are even toxic.

1. What is your assessment of the health of your relationships?
2. Identify changes you need to make.
3. How can you find the courage to make these changes?

EXERCISE #3: NURTURE FRIENDSHIPS

1. Make a list of the actions you have taken over the last three months to nurture supportive friendships.

2. Make a plan to nurture such friendships over the next three months. If needed, make a plan to add a new friend.

3. Consider writing notes of appreciation to friends you value.

4. Schedule time to get together with at least one friend each month.

CHAPTER 8

ZION NATIONAL PARK
AND THE SECRET SERVICE

> *I seldom think about my limitations, and they never make me sad. Perhaps there is a touch of yearning at times; but it is vague, like a breeze among flowers.*
>
> ~ Helen Keller

THE VOICE ON THE PHONE GAVE A SHADOWY EXPLANATION, "I'm sorry I can't tell you who is taking your rooms, but it is a person of national prominence. If you knew who was involved, you'd understand." That certainly piqued my interest and concern.

For the second Wild Women trip, we chose to hike Zion National Park in Utah. The group on the first trip had been comprised of women from the western part of the United States, and me, lovingly called the Wild Woman of the East. Wild Women participation was by invitation only, so for Zion, I asked to have two women from my town join our group. Having two long-term east coast friends on the hike would enrich the experience for all of us.

Given my vow to build my stamina to keep up with the Wild Women on each hike, I had begun to walk and started an exercise routine at our local gym. I set a challenge for myself: be able to hike on the most strenuous trails with the group.

My two east coast friends and I had made reservations a year in advance to room together in one of the cabins near the lodge. When the mysterious phone call came to each of us the night before we were to leave, we were annoyed and then some. What right did the lodge have to allow someone to preempt us? We had made our reservations and paid our deposits. We had a right to our cabin.

The next day, when we arrived, full of complaints, we discovered it was the First Lady, Laura Bush, who had preempted us. She was hiking in Zion National Park with her own set of women friends. Our space had been given to the Secret Service team. What could we say? We moved and hoped to get a glimpse of Mrs. Bush at some point.

We never did cross paths with the First Lady and her friends. The trails they hiked were closed to the rest of us. I'm sure, though, the trails these women hiked were not empty, overrun as they were with security guards. I do hope everyone was acclimated to the altitude.

We did see a hint of the First Lady's entourage when they were leaving the morning of our third day at Zion. We saw men in suits (in a national park?), with hats, sunglasses, and dogs, heading for the SUVs that carried their luggage and supplies.

As for the Wild Women, our first day's hike was to Angel's Landing. This 2.4-mile trail entails a switch back that winds the hiker up the side of Zion and peaks at an altitude of 5790 feet. The route runs along a narrow rock formation, with dizzying drops on both sides, slowly gaining an elevation of about 1500 feet (from 4290 to 5790 feet). The final half mile is strenuous, littered with sharp drop-offs and narrow paths.

Roughly one third of the way up the trail, before reaching a series of switchbacks known as Walter's Wiggles, I realized I was dizzy. No matter how much I had prepared for this trip, the altitude was going to do me in. I hiked for about an hour, then sat down and faced a difficult choice.

I could continue to feel inadequate and persevere along the trail until I harmed myself and held up the rest of the group, or I could accept my limitations, realize I was unable to hike high altitudes, and enjoy what I could comfortably hike each day.

I'd like to believe I cheerfully waved everyone else on as I turned around and hiked back down the mountain. In fact, althhough I hid my true feelings, I wasn't cheerful at all. I wanted desperately to keep up with the rest of the Wild Women. I wanted to conquer the age difference between the rest of the group and myself. I wanted to do myself proud.

As I hiked down the mountain, I was flooded with disappointment and self-blame. I was frustrated that I had discovered hiking late in life. I had missed so much—and now it was too late. I blamed myself for not exercising more, for letting myself be out of shape. My internal gremlins had quite a party beating me up.

In spite of the gremlins, I didn't quite give up. I hiked that day along the Emerald Pools riverbed, which was just as beautiful as the higher altitude hike. I welcomed everyone as the Wild Women trekked back to the lodge.

The hikes on our second and third day at Zion were wonderful. Linda and Lois had physical health issues as well, so we hiked the lower trails within the park. Throughout the days, we had wonderful conversations about life, work, our dreams, and our aspirations. We walked for about an hour, stopping along the way to take pictures, admire the scenery, and simply enjoy the outdoors. The rocks were our chairs when we sat to talk or drink; the beauty of nature was our focus. Nothing else mattered. We didn't care that others in our group were testing their limits of strength and stamina on higher trails.

At the end of each day, when everyone gathered for drinks and hors d'oeuvres before dinner, we all had stories to tell; we all had adventures to share. Linda, Lois, and I had simply seen a different part of the park than the rest. No one treated us differently because we had physical limitations. No one judged us because we had chosen a less demanding route. In fact, the others wanted to know what we had seen, just as we wanted to know what they had seen.

At the slower pace Linda, Lois, and I hiked, we had an additional benefit. We had time to build friendships.

At the end of the Zion trip, I felt far more satisfied than disappointed. While hiking with Linda and Lois, I experienced the beauty of nature at a pace I could manage. On the trails, worlds away from my busy life, I realized I didn't need to "keep up" or compete in impossible situations. I didn't have to be embarrassed about the effect of my age difference with the rest of the Wild Women.

I left Zion National Park believing it is not always important to reach the top of the mountain. Sometimes, it is better simply to do the best you can under the circumstances and let the rest go. It is okay to accept your limitations without embarrassment or self-judgment. When you accept your limitations, others will accept them too.

This was a hard lesson for a competitive and proud individual. The lesson came as the result of a fierce internal struggle. As I left Zion, I believed I had learned the lesson well. Unfortunately, I would have to learn the lesson repeatedly.

> *Don't walk in front of me, I may not follow. Don't walk behind me, I may not lead. Just walk beside me and be my friend.*
>
> ~ Albert Camus

PRINCIPLES TO PROPEL YOU FORWARD

1. When you accept your limitations without embarrassment or self-judgment, others will accept them too.

2. Life is easier when you work from your strengths and accept your limitations.

3. It is not always important to "reach the top." Sometimes it is more important to do the best you can under the current situation and let the rest go.

FROM MY LIFE TO YOURS

A 2008 article in *Time Magazine* starts this way:

> Five years ago, Dr. Alice Domar, a successful psychologist in Boston, had what she describes as an "ah-ha experience." A new patient, whom she refers to as "Kim," came in for an evaluation. Kim seemed to have everything—a happy marriage, four well-adjusted kids, a well-to-do lifestyle, good health and a trim figure. Admits Domar, "As she was telling me her story, I was listening to her thinking, what the hell is she doing seeing me?" It turns out that Kim was distressed by the messiness in her house. She told Domar, "Every time I open a drawer or closet and see the clutter, I feel like a miserable failure."
>
> For Domar, that was a wake-up call about perfectionism. "Women are unhappy because, even if 11 out of

12 things are going well, they zero in on the one that isn't, and they get miserable about it."

At the beginning of our Zion trip, I had the limiting belief that I had to be perfect in everything I did on the hike. I was sure the Wild Women wouldn't like me unless I were perfect in every way. I was convinced I had to hike every trail with the entire group in order to fit in.

In retrospect, of course, that was ridiculous. The belief was false. It turned out that the Wild Women liked me even when I didn't keep up with them. They liked me for who I am.

On that first day at Zion, however, I allowed my limiting beliefs to burden me with unrealistic demands. That first day contained lots of self-judgment and self-blame. I exhausted myself with effort and negative self-talk.

Over the years, I've seen my healthy desire to succeed get mixed up with an unrealistic drive for perfectionism. When it comes to my coaching profession, it's appropriate to go "all out," to learn everything I can and practice every skill. Thanks to some natural ability, good training, and hard work, I'm good at coaching. Unfortunately, I've often suffered under the limiting belief that this means I should be good at everything I try. I have a master's level certification as a coach, plus years of practice. I have neither of these in hiking. Yet, the first day in Zion, I expected master's level performance from myself.

Once I began to change my expectations and realize that Lois and Linda were accepting of their limitations, I could lean back and enjoy the experience of the moment. What a valuable lesson!

EXERCISE #1: EXCELLENCE OR PERFECTIONISM?

Reflect upon your approach to life: Do you pursue excellence (do your best) or strive for perfection (expect yourself to be superhuman)?

In cases when you pursue perfection, identify the price you pay in the process. For example, does the pursuit of perfection lead to anxiety, exhaustion, poor self-esteem, or damaged relationships? Describe in detail the price you pay.

Describe how your life would change if you decreased the power that perfectionism holds over you.

EXERCISE #2: MANIFESTATIONS OF PERFECTIONISM

The urge for perfection leads some people to work excessively to meet self-imposed unrealistic standards. They become workaholics, health and fitness fanatics, etc.

On the other hand, the urge for perfection leads some to a paralysis of procrastination. The fear of not being able to reach their own standards makes them too afraid to try.

1. Explore your own reaction to the urge for perfection.
2. How does the urge for perfection manifest itself in behavior in your life?

EXERCISE #3: EXPOSE LIMITING BELIEFS

To expose your limiting beliefs about perfectionism, complete these sentences with your first response. Don't allow yourself to stop and think.

1. When I do something perfectly, it means I am

   _____.

2. When I fail to do something perfectly, it means I am

   _____.

3. When others see me do something less than perfectly, they think I am _____.

4. If I expose my limitations, people will treat me in the following ways: _____.

5. My need to be perfect began _____.

Next, reflect on these beliefs. In what ways are they valid or invalid?

EXERCISE #4: LET GO

List two areas in your life where you can let perfectionism go. Choose areas in which it is appropriate for you to do your best and enjoy the experience without the burden of perfectionism.

CHAPTER 9

GRAND CANYON, BLOODY LEG, AND WRONG TRAIL SCARE

Do one thing every day that scares you.
~ Eleanor Roosevelt

O N JANUARY 1ST AT 12:01 A.M., I was on the phone attempting to reserve the cabins closest to the rim of the Grand Canyon for our third Wild Women trip. My diligence paid off. When we arrived at our cabins in August, we were within spitting distance of the rim. What a view!

It is said you are in heaven if you can hear the silence. At the North Rim of the Grand Canyon, looking toward the South Rim, you indeed can hear the silence. I have never felt such peace, tranquility, and calm.

As I prepared for this trip, Don's health continued to deteriorate, but thankfully, there were no emergencies or surprises. As was Don's pattern, he loudly protested before resigning himself to my travel plans.

Shortly after the Wild Women trip to Zion, my commitment to accept limitations had somehow gotten lost. In retrospect, it was unwise to expect a lifetime of striving for perfection to undo itself in a single lesson, even if the lesson took place on a mountain.

As I prepared for the trip to the Grand Canyon, I knew that, at 67 years of age, I had a choice: take shorter, easier hikes as I had in the past or try to keep pace with the fittest of the Wild Women, no matter how long or strenuous their hikes. Pushing my lessons from Zion to the back of my mind, I chose the latter.

For this trip, I was determined to be in good physical shape. I worked with a trainer for eight months to build stamina and strength. The result: I completed every hike, every day, while deepening the bonds of friendship. I definitely wasn't the fastest hiker, but I completed every hike.

This trip, like all the Wild Women trips, brought home to me the power of women mentoring and supporting other women. For example, Charlene has a hearing problem and is handicapped without hearing aids. On the first day, Charlene's batteries went dead. No replacements were available. Without any discussion, each of us took the initiative to spend time walking with Charlene. When one person left, another took her place. The women did the same for me.

Always the last to reach the end of the trail, someone consistently slowed down to walk with me. The resulting one-on-one conversations, while hiking on the trails within the context of the entire group, deepened our bonds of friendship. The gesture also made me feel like a precious member of the group.

Even in the context of supportive women, I had a fear of looking down from great heights. One afternoon during the group's quiet time, I decided to tackle this fear by following a path near the lodge that extends from the rim itself and ends on a lookout about 1/4 mile into the gorge. I made it to the end of the path and decided I could go no farther. I was ready to turn around when a woman who was painting on a rock asked,

"Would you like me to take your picture at the end of the look-out?"

Was this serendipity? A coincidence? I swallowed and told her I was afraid, but I would walk the quarter mile to the end of the lookout if she would be patient with me. And, absolutely, "Yes," I wanted a picture of it.

Slowly, I walked to the end, my heart in my throat. I turned around and grasped the rail as this lovely woman took my picture. I did it. With the patience, encouragement, and support of yet another woman, I faced a fear and won. The picture is one of my favorites from this trip.

Now, when I am afraid of doing something, I remember this trip and conquering yet another fear. Then I just go for it. What exhilaration when I step through fear and find it is not so bad on the other side!

By the time we got to the last hike of the Grand Canyon trip, I was feeling confident. According to the maps, this particular hike, called the Kindrick Trail, was about five miles long, circling along the Grand Canyon Rim for most of those miles. The hike was considered only moderately difficult. "I can do this," I said to myself.

The beauty surrounding us was breathtaking. The sky was vibrant blue, and even the rocks wore the colors of the rainbow. We rarely saw other hikers, and the grandeur of the place, the colors, the sense of peace, and the sound of silence took my breath away. Other than our quiet conversations as we trekked up and down the increasingly steep trail and the laughter as we told stories, the only sound we heard was the wind whirling through the Canyon.

As the day moved towards sunset, we continued to hike. By mid-afternoon, I had begun to feel my age and reach my saturation point. As we were climbing up a particularly steep hill, my shoe caught on a fallen tree branch and over I went, on my bum, blood gushing out of my leg. Luckily, Wild Woman Marion was a nurse. Out came the first aid kit to patch me up. Once I caught my breath, we were on our way again.

As we continued to hike for what seemed hours, I was struggling to put one foot in front of the other. Then I overheard the two lead hikers, Andrea and Lois, talking; they were concerned we were on the wrong trail. Even they felt we had surely already hiked five miles.

We stopped to rest and consulted our maps. Perhaps we were on the 10-mile trail. If so, we would need to sleep on the trail as the day was waning and our cars were parked at the 5-mile trailhead. We were uncertain of our location and lacked sleeping bags or warm clothing for the night. Just to be safe, we began to conserve our water and food.

As we hiked, we looked for a place to settle in for the night, one that was relatively safe and could give us warmth as we huddled. In the meantime, our two most experienced hikers stepped up the pace and hiked ahead.

The rest of us felt flutters of fear in our chests, and my legs ached, but as Wild Women, we weren't about to give in to distress or panic. We began to talk about our situation as a great adventure, a story we would tell others when we got back to civilization.

After some time passed, we heard the whistle that told us we were on the right path after all, and the cars were within spitting distance. While we laughed at our own angst, we were also somewhat sad we hadn't gotten stuck on the mountain for a night. We were relieved and missing our bragging rights at the same time.

That night during our nightly wine, hors d'oeuvres, laughter, and conversation, the group toasted me, saying, "Donna, when we get to be your age, we hope we are as strong and adventurous as you are now. You are our role model." They also took pictures of my wounded leg. I was proud of myself. This ole broad was not done yet.

I didn't come home from the Grand Canyon trip with a story of being stuck overnight on a mountain, but I did bring home a scar on my leg. Even today, when I look at that scar, I am reminded of the camaraderie of the group and especially of their acceptance of me and my limitations.

I left that Wild Women trip feeling powerful and refreshed, ready once again to be a caregiver—with both attentiveness and compassion. I NEEDED these trips each year.

The emotional lift from this trip helped prepare me for the year that lay ahead. The time between the Grand Canyon trip and our next trip to Glacier National Park would sorely test my strength as a woman, wife, and mother.

> *Fear is only as deep as the mind allows.*
> ~ Japanese Proverb

PRINCIPLES TO PROPEL YOU FORWARD

1. Acknowledging and then stepping through your fears and self-imposed limitations releases you to live your dreams.

2. You can overcome fears by testing the assumptions behind them and the probability of your fears coming true.

FROM MY LIFE TO YOURS

For the trip to the North Rim of the Grand Canyon, I forgot the hard-learned lesson from Zion of accepting my limitations. For this trip, my training and perseverance paid off, and I was able to keep up with the group, even though I was consistently at the end of the pack.

Unfortunately, things wouldn't necessarily turn out this way in future years. I would have to learn the lesson about accepting my limitations repeatedly. This lesson is a theme that runs throughout my journey toward living large.

Another theme is the need to face my fears. According to a 2009 issue of *Psychology Today*,

> Fear is a vital response to physical and emotional danger—if we didn't feel it, we couldn't protect ourselves from legitimate threats. Trauma or bad experiences can trigger a fear response within us that is hard to quell. People can also develop specific fears as a result of learning. But often we fear situations that are far from life-or-death, and thus we hold back from life situations for no good reason.

To overcome our fears, we again have to test our assumptions about our own life situations. For example, as I gingerly walked and talked myself to the end of the overlook in the Grand Canyon, I tested some basic assumptions:

> *Assumption:* I was profoundly afraid I would fall over the edge into the Canyon.
>
> *Reality:* There was probably less than a 5% chance I would fall as long as I held onto the railing at the edge.
>
> *Assumption:* I was sure the overlook would collapse as I went close to the edge.
>
> *Reality:* That railing had been there a long time, and it looked solid. There was probably less than a 5% chance it would collapse.

EXERCISE #1: WHAT WOULD YOU LOVE TO DO?

Identify one thing you would truly LOVE to do but don't because you are afraid to fail. How often do you tell yourself you cannot do this? Complete this sentence:

Because I'm___(example: too heavy)_____,
I cannot ___(example: climb this mountain)_____.

Because I'm_____,
I cannot_____:

EXERCISE #2: COME TO THE EDGE

The following poem by Christopher Logue is one of my favorites:

Come to the edge.
We might fall.
Come to the edge.
It's too high!
COME TO THE EDGE!
And they came,
and he pushed,
And they flew.

With the poem in mind, answer the following questions:

1. What is your personal edge you are afraid to peer over?
2. What is the assumption (limiting belief) behind your fear?
3. What is the probability of your fear coming true?
4. What are the possibilities if you went to the edge, looked over, and flew?
5. What does flying look like for you?
6. How could someone in your support group help you step through your fear?

CHAPTER 10

GLACIER NATIONAL PARK, DEATH, AND LAUGHTER

Live with intention.

Walk to the edge.

Listen hard.

Practice wellness.

Play with abandon.

Laugh.

Choose with no regret.

Appreciate your friends.

Continue to learn.

Do what you love.

Live as if this is all there is.

~ Mary Anne Radmacher

N EAR THE END OF DECEMBER EACH YEAR, as part of a holiday gift to clients, friends, and colleagues, I send out an exercise to help people reflect on the past and prepare for the upcoming year. The exercise guides participants to list their breakthroughs and breakdowns for the past year. It guides them to identify what they need to do to let go of the past and move forward.

My favorite part of the exercise is the task to name the year ahead. This task allows the participant to set an intention and tone for the coming year. (Complete instructions are at the end of this chapter.)

By December of 2008, I had developed a specialty in my coaching practice. While I called myself an executive coach, it seemed I had a gift for attracting and empowering women in transition with one-on-one coaching. I had successfully conducted two weekend retreats for women in transition that year, using a journal I designed as well as one of Joan Anderson's books, *A Weekend to Change Your Life*, as a template. With the success of these two retreats, I felt on top of the world. Thus, at my 68th year, I chose to name my upcoming year, *Laugh and Dance with Spirit.*

Throughout the ensuing year, I felt as though I had misnamed my year for the first time. By the time I reached the Wild Women trip in Glacier National Park that summer, I was depleted and felt as if I had no laugher or spirit left in me. I felt betrayed by life.

Between January 1st and the day I left for our Glacier trip, I experienced three significant deaths. Jamie, in a relationship with a woman he was unlikely to marry, took responsibility for an unplanned pregnancy. He was ready to be a father, and I was looking forward to being a grandmother.

My grandson, the only biological one I am likely to have, was born at 6-1/2 months gestation and lived a total of 10 hours. My own loss, as well as the agony of being a support person for my son and the mother of his child, drained all the energy and spirit within me.

At the same time, I was the daily companion of a neighbor and precious friend who was dying of melanoma. I was also regularly visiting a dear colleague who was dying of a brain tumor.

Each of these deaths occurred roughly within a month of each other. All that, and I was still caregiver for my husband. Don's health grew progressively worse as the months went by. He was needy and demanding. It was not a season of laughter.

Many times throughout that year, I found my faith being severely tested. In future years, as I looked back on this time, I often wondered what got me through. Now I know that a number of things fortified me, including my faith in a supreme being and my faith in my own resiliency. My experience on Machu Picchu, where I survived by taking one step at a time, underscored my belief that grit and determination would see me through. And my wonderful women friends, from various facets of my life, were there for me.

Workwise, I received a refreshing challenge. The Dean and Assistant Dean at Duquesne University School of Leadership and Professional Advancement asked me to consider putting together a coach certification program. At the moment I was asked, all I could think of was, "Yes, it sounds like a fun project."

With years of experience coaching both external and internal to organizations, as well as in my own one-on-one coaching practice, I was uniquely qualified to develop a formal coach certification program.

I had a choice between two directions approved by the International Coach Federation (ICF). I could develop a program of Approved Coach Specific Training Hours (ACSTH) or an Accredited Coach Training Program (ACTP).

The difference between the two programs is in the content and time required. The ACTP includes an additional 95 hours of core training for participants, a coach supervision component, and a written exam approved by the ICF. Undaunted by the requirements, I decided on the ACTP program and dove right in.

When asked to develop the coach certification program, I knew that as founder and architect of such a program at Duquesne, I'd gain additional credibility and recognition. In addition, the program could serve as my legacy as I moved out of full-time work and into retirement. This opportunity seemed to provide a great outlet for positive energy in a very dark time.

As I said, "Yes," however, I had no idea of the mass of paperwork and time that would encroach upon my life before we were granted official status as a bona fide coach training program for ICF. Later, I would discover that it takes most ACTP programs a minimum of two years to develop the program. My team took nine months. We were officially approved by the ICF in a little over two years.

By the time I checked into the Many Lodge in Glacier National Park for the Wild Women trip, all I wanted to do was stay in my room and sleep for days. I did not want to hike. I did not want to talk with a single soul.

The universe must have known I needed some silence and space because my room was at the opposite end of the lodge, away from all the other Wild Women. Ann, my usual traveling partner, did not come on this trip, so I had a single room. I also had a small porch with a wonderful view of the glaciers and a lake.

In spite of my exhaustion, I felt I belonged on the trip, and that my role this time was to listen deeply to others. More importantly, I needed to listen deeply to my own inner voice. I needed to take time to mourn the deaths of my grandson and my friends. Also at this point, I was considering writing this book and needed to understand my reasons for doing so. What was so special about my life that others continued to ask me to write my stories?

In contrast to the previous year when I had worked so hard to be physically prepared to keep up with the Wild Women, I had neither the desire nor need to keep up. I purposefully chose to reflect and rest instead of hiking every day. Each of the women understood and gave me space.

This Wild Women trip had a completely different flavor. For once, I wasn't striving, competing, or pushing myself to keep up, and it was wonderful. The Wild Women enveloped me into their hearts. They gave me the space I needed to grieve, listened to me without comment, and accepted that for this year I was not going to be the cheerful, always-laughing Donna. I felt validated for who I was: the older, key member of the group as well as a hiker who tried like hell to keep up with them, whether she could or not. I learned a profound lesson: sometimes it is okay to be the one taken care of.

One day during this trip, instead of hiking with the women, I sat on the lodge patio, rocking, drinking coffee, and writing in my journal. By listening to what my body and spirit needed, rather than pushing myself to keep up with the others, I was able to let go of some of my grief and see my path forward.

As I reflected, I saw that through the past months laughter had been present; it just was not the kind of laughter I was used to. My dear friend, Cheryl, who died of melanoma, had great spirit. Cheryl shared her spirit and love of life with all of us who were with her to the end.

When I took Cheryl to chemotherapy sessions or sat with her when she was too weak to get out of bed, we talked and laughed about life, about the men in our lives, about everything and anything. Our spirits laughed and danced in the midst of suffering and sadness. My year had not been incorrectly named after all.

In retrospect, I think this Wild Women trip offered the most learning of them all. For the first time in my entire life, I didn't try to compete or keep up with others. For the first time, I didn't measure up. I was too tired to make the effort to be perfect, to be the leader, and to be there for everyone else. To my great surprise, it was okay. It turned out that, at least as far as the Wild Women went, my lofty expectations were self-inflicted. The Wild Women simply expected me to be present and be my authentic self. They valued me as a person, not an achiever. In short, they loved me.

> *As the ancient Indian sages observed thousands of years ago, our destiny is shaped by the deepest level of our intention and desire. Once we plant the seed of an intention in the fertile ground of pure potentiality, our soul's journey unfolds automatically, as naturally as a bulb becomes a tulip or an embryo becomes a child.*
> ~ Chopra Center Website

PRINCIPLES TO PROPEL YOU FORWARD

1. You can set intentions to release power to live on your own terms (see below).
2. You can have laughter and spirit in the midst of deep personal pain or loss.
3. Some of the deepest, most profound life lessons come from being quiet and restful.

FROM MY LIFE TO YOURS

Each year, I carefully work through my "end of year" exercise. I devote time and energy to this task for two reasons:

1. I want to learn from my successes and failures over the past year.

2. I want to set an intention to guide the year I'm entering.

Intentions are powerful, and naming your year is one way to set an intention for what's ahead. Intentions continue to work in your life, even when you are not consciously thinking of them.

My 2009 name, *Laugh and Dance with Spirit*, had a positive significance on my life in unexpected ways. It sustained me and gave me the oomph I needed to get through some difficult life challenges.

In 2010, I named my year, *Rethink*. For 2011, I chose the name, *Year of Synthesis*. For 2012, I took the name, *The Year to Enjoy What IS*. For 2013, as I write, I've chosen the name, *If Not Now, When?*

As you think about your own intentions, the following words from Sharon Salzberg published in 2004 in *O* (The Oprah Magazine), might be helpful:

> I recently attended a yoga retreat where I was the rank (and awfully timid) novice. Every other student in our class was far more limber, easily flowing into pretzel-like poses. Almost worse, they all seemed to know the traditional Sanskrit name for each move.
>
> One day as my teacher, John Friend, was demonstrating a pose, he made an awkward-looking movement, then rebalanced. Coming out of it he asked, "What just happened?" One by one, my classmates offered a Sanskrit name for that extra little twist. Finally, John turned to me and repeated his question, "What just happened?" I replied, "To be honest, I think you fell." "You're right," he said. "I fell. Then I started over. That's good yoga."

I have always regarded John as a wonderful teacher, and I think of that incident as one of his very best lessons. It was about honoring the role of intention, the heart space that guides everything we undertake. If we fall, we don't need self-recrimination or blame or anger—we need a reawakening of our intention and a willingness to recommit, to be wholehearted once again.

Often we can achieve an even better result when we stumble yet are willing to start over, when we don't give up after a mistake, when something doesn't come easily but we throw ourselves into trying, when we're not afraid to appear less than perfectly polished. By prizing heartfulness above faultlessness, we may reap more from our effort because we're more likely to be changed by it. We learn and grow and are transformed not so much by what we do but by why and how we do it.

Intention is not just about will—or about resolutions we make on New Year's Eve with shaky hope in our hearts—but about our overall everyday vision, what we long for, what we believe is possible for us. If we want to know the spirit of our activities, the emotional tone of our efforts, we have to look at our intentions.

EXERCISE: END OF YEAR

Here is my traditional end-of-the-year exercise. Take some time just for you. Reflect. Pause. Look at what you've accomplished—or not—and let what you discover guide you positively through this coming year.

STEP ONE

Look over the past year (or other period):

1. Make a list of all the wins, successes, and breakthroughs in the past year. Look at all areas of your life, not just your professional life.

2. Make a list of all the losses, disappointments, and breakdowns in the past year.

3. Ask yourself what it means to be "complete" in each circumstance. Incompleteness holds us back from taking on the next exciting opportunity.

STEP TWO

Looking over the past year, what are the two or three lessons you have learned unequivocally? Choose the lessons you want to carry over into the New Year. Some examples:

- I learned to be in the moment and trust that the universe knows what is in store for me.

- I learned that my mistakes do not mean I am a failure.

- I learned how precious life is and to enjoy every moment.

STEP THREE

Imagine one year ahead, and write a list of all the wins, successes, and breakthroughs for the coming year. What would you like to learn or accomplish by the end of the next year? Write this list as though it has already happened. Make it as long as you choose, and be sure to look at each area of your life.

Prioritize your list. Look at how each item fits with your values. Make plans and set accountability for the next year.

STEP FOUR

Much like the Chinese tradition that gives names to each year, choose a name for this coming year. Use images, symbols, or other signs to name the coming year. Choose an image that allows you to step more fully into who you want to be and are already becoming. Find a name that stretches your imagination and moves you into greater possibility. Examples from my past years and those of my clients, colleagues, and friends include the following:

- *Strong Alone*

- *Year of the Wild Woman Set Free*

- *My Non-Year*

- *Listen to My Inner Voice*

- *Reach for the Unreachable*

- *I Can Do This!*

I find this is the hardest part of the exercise—but when I give the year a name, that name can be a clear and distinct intention that really guides my year! Let your intuition be your guide.

Let your mind run wild while you are skiing, sitting by the fire, or watching football over the holidays.

What will you name your year?

CHAPTER 11

OVERWORK AND
HOSPITAL BEDS

> *Courage doesn't always roar. Sometimes courage is the little voice at the end of the day that says, "I'll try again tomorrow."*
>
> ~ Mary Anne Radmacher

THE JANUARY FOLLOWING THE Wild Women trip to Glacier National Park, I found myself, at 69 years old, working harder and longer than I had in my younger years. I had dived headfirst into the task of designing, developing, and directing the coach certification training program for Duquesne University.

As I mentioned earlier, I had committed to obtaining the International Coach Federation's (ICF) Accredited Coach Training Program (ACTP) designation, which is the more rigorous of the two options. What's more, I had committed to complete the task with an ambitious schedule. We were just a few months from being accepted as an official coach training program with the ICF. The project was progressing, our cohort-based groups were full, and the program was gaining credibility in the coaching community.

As the New Year rolled in, my weariness forced the following questions: What is wrong with this picture? What is propelling me to continue at this heavy pace?

On one level, I was working hard because I loved what I was doing and believed it was worthwhile. Working with students and overcoming administrative obstacles gave me a sense of satisfaction. Developing a program that could help generations of aspiring coaches imbued my life with meaning.

On another level, working hard kept me from becoming depressed over my husband's ever-worsening health. After 10 years of illness, Don continued to decline but at an excruciatingly slow pace. At this point, Don was cranky, critical, and not particularly grateful for my help. A thankless job awaited me daily at home. And, no matter where I was or what I was doing, I felt the strain of expecting a phone call indicating an emergency or death. In the midst of the strain, Duquesne was a place where I felt good, where I was respected and appreciated. What's more, I had some control over my work when I had little control over other areas of my life. Yet, the combination of caretaking and working long hours was exhausting. I was out of balance.

In the early spring of that year, seeking renewal, I took myself out of my routine by spending a few days in the mountains nearby. I took my wonderful companion, Magoo (a miniature schnauzer), with me and rented a cabin in the woods in nearby Clarion County. My plan was to write, read, and relax. I also planned to kayak on the Clarion River. I had good memories of kayaking in the park near my home, in the bay on Cape May, and on the Allegheny River. In each of these places, the water was smooth and the experience pleasant.

As planned, I headed down to the river, talked to the outfitters, asked all kinds of questions: Was it safe to paddle alone?

What happened if I hit a rock? What about the little rapids I saw on the river? On and on.

The outfitters assured me I'd be fine paddling alone, that the river was so low that I couldn't possibly hurt myself or drown. So I paid my money, rented the kayak, and accepted a ride upstream to the drop-off point.

Along the way, my heart was in my throat. What was I doing? I was alone. I was too old for this. I looked at those little rapids and wondered how I would get around them. Perhaps I should just ride back to the outfitter station with the driver and forget it. On and on churned my worrisome thoughts.

Finally, we reached the drop-off point. "Okay, Donna," I thought, "play large; just get in the damn boat and paddle. You will be okay." I did and I was.

Paddling around the first ripple in the river (which indicated a large rock or boulder beneath the surface) was scary, but I made it through. The second ripple was a bit larger, but I made it around that one safely, too. "Hey," I thought, "this is fun." For the rest of the five miles, I anticipated the ripples, looked forward to them, and enjoyed the ride. I ended up wishing the river were a bit more exciting.

Reflecting on the day, I saw the experience as another metaphor for my life and for the woman I was becoming. Although I might be frightened when faced with a difficult and potentially scary new adventure, I no longer held back or gave in to my fear. And one hundred percent of the time, I passed through that fear just fine, wishing I had moved forward earlier. I liked this new person.

Soon after this trip to the Clarion River, my health took a nosedive. In retrospect, I had not been feeling well for several months but, typical for me, I had ignored my symptoms. I attributed the lower back pain I began to feel to my kayak trip on the Clarion. Then I developed shingles, which I attributed to working long hours for the coach program as well as taking care of my husband.

The universe was sending me a message; I was not listening. My health continued to nosedive until one day the universe got through to me. Totally out of character for me, after taking care of my husband's needs for the day, I said, "I don't feel well and am going to the Emergency Room." I don't know where that intuition came from; I'm thankful I followed it. I probably would have died if I hadn't taken myself to the hospital that day.

At the hospital, I was diagnosed with a pulmonary infarction/embolism. This means I had dangerous blood clots in my lungs—and potential lung tissue death as a result. While I was released from the hospital six days later on blood thinning medication, healing was an entirely different matter. Healing required the next six months.

While I had spent the few years prior to this illness conditioning to hike in the mountains, I was now working hard to walk down my driveway. Making my way to the end of my street and back was now a gargantuan task. The healing was slow—painfully slow.

One of my biggest disappointments during this time was that I was unable to attend a Wild Women trip. I hadn't missed a single one since the beginning.

Because of the blood thinners and my still-delicate health, my doctor did not want me flying. Of course, I tried to tell the doctor I would be okay, but when he learned this year's trip was to a remote mountainous area, many miles from the nearest hospital, the doctor said, "NO, Donna. Period." I gave up for that particular year, but I felt the loss acutely.

While my body healed, my mind worked overtime. I had almost lost my life. If I had died, would I have been happy with what I had accomplished? In the face of the fragility of life, what did I want to continue doing? What did I no longer want to do? What passion was strong enough to merit my energy? What legacy did I want to leave when I finally did pass on? With fresh knowledge that life is short, I asked myself what I wanted to do with the time I had left.

While the questions were many, the answers were very clear. I remembered Frankie, the woman in her 70s who had so impressed me on the Isle of Iona. Here I was, approaching Frankie's age at the time of our meeting, and I was struggling with a serious illness.

I held to Frankie's example, determined not to give in to sadness and stop living simply because I was aging and adjusting to health limitations. Instead, I spent time clarifying what was important to me then—and what is still important today.

I am passionate about having unique adventures that no one else has. I want to live fully and enjoy the present, every single day. I want to be a role model for women who are stuck in their routines and living small rather than large because they think they have no other choice. I want to be defined by who I am and what I do for others and myself. I do not want to be defined only as someone's caregiver.

Even before my release from the hospital, I decided upon my next adventure. If I survived, I would visit one of my former coaching clients and her family in Japan. Then, the universe stepped in to confirm my plan. Not two weeks after my release from the hospital, I got an e-mail from Chie, asking me when I was coming to Japan to visit.

During my long recovery, I made travel plans for the following April when the cherry blossoms would be blooming in Japan. I had another unique experience to look forward to.

The difficulty of healing was exacerbated by Don's attitude. He seemed to have no patience for the fact that I needed attention and care. When I returned from the hospital, my brother and sister came to help, and Don was angry with Jamie for having called them.

I was devastated at Don's lack of concern and care for me in the face of a life-threatening illness. Having tried so hard to be faithful and meet Don's needs while I tried to live a full life, I was stunned. In the face of Don's downright nastiness, I sobbed and sobbed. I finally accepted that my marriage was over. There was no longer anything between Don and me.

In the face of this realization, I decided to take advice that had been coming my way for years. Before my mother died several years before my illness, she had encouraged me to find someone to date. Jamie, who knew my relationship with Don better than anyone, regularly told me I should date. My friends encouraged me to go online and find someone.

Out of loyalty to Don and my sense of marital commitment, I had ignored the advice for years. Suddenly, I faced what everyone near to me already knew: The marriage was over. While I decided to continue as caretaker for Don, I also decided I was free to pursue another relationship.

Don and I had been married for 40 years, but we had been more like roommates than partners for more years than I could count. Still, I had been out of the dating scene for 40 years. I was 69 years old; who would want to date me? Could I really pursue the dream of a companion, fulfill a longing I'd had for over a decade? Could I find the courage to overcome my fear?

After much soul searching and continued encouragement from my circle of supporters, I decided to go on eHarmony and see what happened. The decision was a natural consequence of my commitment to live on my own terms, having unique adventures.

The whole process of filling out my eHarmony profile felt so foreign that I had to ask Jamie for help. It was bizarre to have my son help me describe myself for dating purposes. Jamie and I worked together, expressing my desire for someone with whom to share my life, a companion for unique adventures and cultural activities, a person with whom I could laugh.

I checked the box that most closely fit my status: widow. Then I hit "submit," having no idea what would come next.

> *Don't try to comprehend with your mind. Your minds are very limited. Use your intuition.*
> ~ Madeline L'Engle

PRINCIPLES TO PROPEL YOU FORWARD

1. In the face of the fragility of life, be clear about what things really matter to you.
2. Your body sends you messages for a reason. Listen to them.
3. You have a right to define yourself as the person you are, not only as one who exists in relationship to others.

FROM MY LIFE TO YOURS

Prior to my illness, my intuition and body were sending me messages meant for my good. I lived with the sense I was working too hard, but I didn't do anything about it. I attributed my back pain to exercise (kayaking) rather than checking with a doctor. I made excuses rather than listen to my intuition and body.

Women are prone to put their physical and emotional needs last on their list of priorities, especially when they are in a role of caring for children, a husband, or parents. Women also tend to be super-responsible. They allow work and volunteer demands to crowd out the need for rest and renewal.

Yet, no one can ignore the need to rest and renew indefinitely without paying serious consequences.

Here are five suggestions for relaxing, renewing, and rejuvenating:

1. *Realize your work and play rhythms.* When it's time to work, do so with gusto and enjoyment. When it's time to play, do the same. If you are not accustomed to playing, be patient with yourself. Begin by deciding what activities you find most invigorating, and incorporate these into your schedule. For example, schedule the time to ride your bike along a trail for 45 minutes several days a week, visit a museum once a month, or take a leisurely stroll on your lunch hour with someone you enjoy.

2. *Tune out and turn inward.* Seek to build consistent quiet and reflection time into your daily routine. During this time, do not check e-mail, receive or place phone calls, answer questions, or interact with anyone. Instead, turn inward by choosing a quiet spot where you can sit and listen to your own breathing. It may take a while to tune out, but with practice, you can develop a quiet, calming routine that lends itself to personal renewal.

3. *Learn to say "No."* If you find saying "No" difficult, remind yourself that when you say "Yes" to something you'd rather not do, you're automatically saying "No" to something you might be good at and enjoy.

4. *Remind yourself that an exhaustive to-do list does not equal fulfillment.* When we lose touch with our creative, playful selves, our lives may feel empty. Many times, we try to fill that emptiness with activities that distract us but don't offer meaning. Scrutinize your to-do list with

CHAPTER 12

eHARMONY AND THINKING OF RETIREMENT

> *Your assumptions are your windows on the world.*
> *Scrub them off every once in awhile, or the light won't*
> *come in.*
>
> ~ Alan Alda

WHEN eHARMONY SENT ME PROFILES, I felt an odd mix of emotions. Anticipating any date at all, let alone making a choice electronically, seemed surreal. I interacted with a number of men via e-mail. In the end, the profile of only one man, Glenn, beckoned to me. Glenn and I e-mailed back and forth, talked, and finally met for breakfast. During that meal, we talked for 2-1/2 hours with an easy, natural give and take. I liked him.

Glenn shared some of his past with me, including the fact that he was a widower who had lost the love of his life. I could tell Glenn's grief and longing went deep. For my part, I waited until it seemed likely we would meet a second time before I cleared my throat and launched into my awkward admission. "Glenn," I said, "before we decide to take this any further, there's something about me you should know."

I explained that, as a caregiver for 12 years, I was a widow in a practical, if not a literal, sense. I explained that my son and the other significant people in my life had been encouraging me to date for years. I explained that while I would care for Don until his death, I no longer wanted to sacrifice my right to a companion.

As I conveyed this information in a manner I hoped would give him room to escape as well as to accept an unconventional relationship, Glenn listened carefully. He chose the latter, and thus began a completely new adventure in my life.

The beginning of this relationship had its challenges as I struggled with feelings of guilt. Mentally, I chose to proceed, knowing I was living as faithfully to Don as I was able, knowing I had a right to a full life. I was defining my own role rather than allowing society to define my marital obligations. Still, guilt sometimes pierced my peace.

I also struggled with what to expect of the relationship. Glenn was only looking for someone with whom to share cultural experiences. I wanted someone with whom to share my life as well as to join me as a companion on my adventures. Often, I felt Glenn's first wife between us, as I'm sure he often felt Don's presence.

Glenn and I talked openly about our relationship and accepted each other as we were. I discovered that Glenn was a wonderful man who shared my interests and was eager to introduce me to new, unique adventures. These included weekend canoe and camping trips as well as travels to different national parks, including Dry Tortugas, which is 70 miles off the Florida Keys. As a widower, Glenn knew about, understood, and was supportive of what I was doing as a caregiver.

With Glenn in my life, things changed for the better. My health improved dramatically, and I found myself more peaceful and compassionate in my relationship with Don. I stopped referring to myself as caregiver and began to envision myself as a re-wired retiree who was still vital and active in work, while enjoying life. Oh yes, and by the way, I was also a dedicated caregiver to my husband.

Even as I was attempting to redefine myself as a retiree with a balanced life, I was still working long hours, especially in the coach certification program at Duquesne. I had once again set nearly impossible demands upon myself, looking for approval from the various perfectionists in my life.

Growing up, everything my five siblings and I did met with disapproval. To this day, I remember a time when, at 16 years old, I cleaned the entire house, hoping to impress my mother. I swept, dusted, re-swept floors, and re-dusted furniture. I was exhausted but pleased with the outcome. The house was spotless.

When Mother walked into the house, I waited with baited breath for her to notice and compliment me on my hard work. Instead, she pointed out a small piece of thread on the floor and reprimanded me for missing it. Mother didn't notice anything but that small piece of thread. To this day, I remember that moment.

I continued to try to please Mother and was disappointed when it didn't happen. Only when Mother died did I realize she had always been proud of me.

In the meantime, I married a man who demanded perfection at all times. Over a 40-year period, while trying to gain approval from a mother who lived many miles away, I was also trying to be perfect for my husband. In addition, being a woman of the 60s (a baby boomer/traditionalist), I believed I had to work harder than men did to get ahead in business. No wonder I ended up in the hospital. I exhausted myself by perpetually trying to gain approval from others.

This theme of perfection was a thread woven into every area of my life. No wonder I became a workaholic, unable to relax and enjoy life as it was happening. Even as I attempted to enjoy my companionship with Glenn, I felt the tension between my chosen approach to life and the workaholic habits of a lifetime. And these habits were strong, even after all the soul searching I had done because of my illness.

Once again, I began testing assumption after assumption. What was I trying to prove by working long hours? What was important to me? What was no longer important? What was I holding on to from my past that simply no longer had any meaning?

Little by little, I removed the clutter from my life, but it wasn't easy. One by one, I resigned from my seats on boards of directors. I reevaluated friendships and acquaintances, and slowly withdrew from those that drained my energy.

I had to remind myself that I never intended to stay in a leadership role at Duquesne. I intended to work hard to establish the program and then leave others to run it. I began to realize I simply didn't have the energy to do everything I was doing, but I found it difficult to move forward. One day I was ready to let go; the next I was in there taking charge and totally confusing my colleagues. Finally, a friend made me tackle the foundational assumption with which I was living.

Here's the assumption, the limiting belief that frightened and tormented me: If I were to retire, I would fade into oblivion. After all, isn't this what happens when people retire? They wither away. I'd seen it happen to my mother and I'd seen it happen to Don.

Retirement was a big, scary, threatening prospect. My identity had always been tied to my work, my projects, and my coaching. Who would I be without a career and work? What would I do with my time? The compelling need to prove my worth by work and achievement was slow to release its grip.

As I was honest with myself and faced my fear, the threads that made up my life began to unravel and reknit themselves into a new, unique experience. Even when I began to let go of control at Duquesne, I found plenty of meaning in my life. Clients came to me for coaching because of where I was in life. Clients asked me to coach them into retirement.

In 2012, I named my year, *The Year to Enjoy What IS*. I attempted to do just that. The need to achieve still pulled at me, and I frequently had to remind myself it was okay to relax and enjoy each day as it came. Looking at the whole, however, I knew I was winning. Life wasn't necessarily easy, but it was good, full of richness and joy.

> *Don't build roadblocks out of assumptions.*
> ~ Lorie Myers

PRINCIPLES TO PROPEL YOU FORWARD

1. Living large requires testing assumptions from childhood that pervade adult life.
2. In order to live fully, de-clutter and eliminate things from your life that don't serve your vision.

FROM MY LIFE TO YOURS

The assumptions underlying most of my life were as follows:

1. I had to be perfect to be accepted.
2. Without work, I would lose my identity.

It wasn't until I tested those assumptions and realized they were invalid that I could break through and chart my life in a different way.

Once, while vacationing in Florida with a friend, I saw the power of childhood assumptions in action. Knowing my friend loved anything sweet, I purchased cookies and left them on the counter.

After three days, those cookies were still there, unopened. When I asked my friend why she had not opened the package, she told me she was waiting for me to open them. Growing up, no one was allowed to eat a cookie until Mother opened the package.

We laughed at the situation; I told my friend she could choose to open the cookies or let them get stale, unopened. There was no mother on vacation with us.

EXERCISE #1: IDENTIFYING CHILDHOOD ASSUMPTIONS

Reflect on the messages and models you received in childhood that turned into assumptions and limiting beliefs about life.

1. Write about your feelings surrounding deserving love. In childhood, did you have to earn love or was it given unconditionally? What assumptions about deserving love did you carry into adulthood? What messages do your gremlins give you about this today?

2. Write about your feelings around work. What messages did you receive regarding work in childhood? What did your parents model? What messages do your gremlins give you today?

3. Write about your feelings around taking time for yourself and/or playing. What messages did you receive regarding self-care and play in childhood? What did your parents model? What messages do your gremlins give you today?

4. Test the validity of each assumption you've identified. Revise your assumptions to match your reality as an adult.

EXERCISE #2: ELIMINATE SELF-IMPOSED CLUTTER

1. Make a list of your activities and obligations that do not serve your vision.

2. Determine which of these constitute self-imposed clutter in your life.

3. Make a plan to eliminate the top offenders.

CHAPTER 13

DEATH VALLEY AND MAKING MOVES

Stepping onto a brand new path is difficult, but not more difficult than remaining in a situation, which is not nurturing to the whole woman.

~ Maya Angelou

IN MARCH OF 2011, JAPAN WAS HIT BY A TSUNAMI, and I had to cancel the trip I had been so looking forward to. At the same time, Don's health deteriorated to the point it was time to call hospice. Don was extremely sick, and I was sure it was finally his time to die. I began to prepare myself for my next steps in life.

Surprising everyone, Don rallied and hospice dismissed him. I couldn't believe it: Don was so stubborn that he failed hospice! Who does that? Don was homebound, mean, and demanding, yet something in him was still determined to live.

With this turn of events, I fell into a deep depression. I wondered if this ordeal with Don would ever end. My role as a caregiver had gone on for so long, with so little thanks, that I was depleted emotionally and physically. In spite of my best intentions, I wanted Don to die. I wanted the struggle to end. I felt tremendous guilt for these feelings and struggled to find a balance.

While Don had rallied, he didn't really improve. As he needed increasingly more care, I began to research retirement communities. In June, I showed Don a brochure for a lovely community called Sherwood Oaks. I was shocked when he consented to visit and then more shocked when he consented to move. Finally, Don would have his needs met, and I would have space to call my own. While Don would still need my care, my role would be less consuming, at least so I thought.

Don's demeanor and financial decisions didn't make the transition easy for me. In fact, I had to sell our home, sort through Don's things as well as my own, and move us both in a matter of a few months. While Don accepted the change, he was angry, mean, and demanding throughout. I soldiered on, exhausted. With the help of Jamie and some supportive friends, I handled all the practical tasks.

In August, I moved Don to an efficiency apartment at Sherwood Oaks. On a day in September, I attended back-to-back closings and moved myself into a lovely townhouse. The following day, with my possessions still in boxes, I was off to Olympic National Park with the Wild Women.

This trip was smaller than the previous ones, with only six of us hiking. Four of us hiked together slowly while two were more aggressive. This Wild Women trip was a gift of refreshment in a time that was largely an exhausted blur. Looking back, I'm not sure how I made it through.

In the months that followed, I was fully aware that my husband was in the final stages of living. Yet, given Don's health history, it seemed those final days might last forever. In the meantime, I maintained my commitment to support and care for Don as well as my commitment to live large in my own life. I continued coaching clients, assumed a lesser role at Duquesne, and continued my relationship with Glenn. The balance was never easy, but I was determined to keep the commitment to myself as well as to Don.

Christmas and New Year's Day came and went, and February dawned with yet another Wild Women trip, my sixth trip with the group over the course of seven years. I arrived in Death Valley, California, with no expectations, perhaps because I had fully expected a crisis with Don to keep me at home.

Sitting on the balcony of my cabin the first day in Death Valley, I had the sense this might be my last trip with this group. After driving 120 miles into the desolate desert to meet up with the Wild Women, I decided the trip would be a success if I hiked as much as I could, laughed in the evenings, and said my final goodbye to the group. I would tell these women how much their friendship had meant to me over the past seven years as I transitioned from an unhappily married caregiver to my present state of living life on my own terms.

As the trip unfolded, I realized I wasn't the only one who felt a change. This whole trip had a different feel. In the evenings, our conversations were especially deep, perhaps because the setting of Death Valley prompted us to talk of our fear of death. We talked about our individual purposes in life, whether each of us knew her purpose, and whether we lived accordingly. One of the women, Charlene, struggled with the question because she was not naturally self-reflective. She didn't know her purpose. Oddly, the rest of us clearly saw joyfully living as her purpose. It was fun to see Charlene's eyes light up as our community affirmed this in her.

I've always thought my specific contribution to the Wild Women was my expertise at asking questions and gently and intuitively pulling the answers from others. I'm a good listener and facilitator. Sometimes, however, I use this strength as a cop out. I listen attentively to others when I am feeling inadequate and small. I hide behind questions rather than take the risk of saying what I truly believe.

Sure enough, when it came time to share my own purpose, I choked up. This group, however, was not about to let me off the hook. They waited for me to respond. Finally, I said, "My absolute passion and purpose is to be a role model for other women as they recognize and step into their own power."

It was wonderful to say this aloud and know it was true. Once I choked out my purpose, I could begin to relate stories from many of my clients, friends, niece, nephew, and others who have been interspersed throughout my life.

I also acknowledged that the Wild Women trips had been one of many ways in which I had run away from my life. How incredible to realize I no longer needed to escape! Chances are this was one of the reasons I was having ambivalent feelings about continuing to participate in these yearly trips.

The women talked about what the Wild Women trips had meant to each of us. We talked about how we had seen each other grow heavier and thinner. While no one died or divorced, one of us (me) let go of an unhealthy marriage and found someone new with whom to share life. Another woman found the love of her life and married. We had survived crises and illnesses. Over the years, we had all looked forward to our times together.

As we had changed and grown, however, the purpose of coming together was also changing for each of us. Andrea, our founder and leader, wanted things to remain the way she designed them: mornings with a shared breakfast and discussion of the hikes we'd tackle that day; the hikes themselves; quiet time; and back together for cocktails and conversation. Unfortunately, it seemed not everyone shared Andrea's vision. Different women were now coming to the group for different reasons.

Some were seeking quiet time to reflect; others were savoring the relationships; still others were coming primarily for the rigors of hiking.

The group, as originally designed, had served an important purpose for seven years, and perhaps now it was time to change. Some women no longer felt the need for the group. Others wanted to change the structure.

As members of the group expressed their opinions, I saw how painful the discussion was for Andrea. She had poured her heart into realizing her vision for this group, and now we were telling her we no longer shared the vision. We wanted something different. It hurt. I could see that, for Andrea, this stung like a betrayal.

Of course, the Wild Women were not pursuing change for its own sake, nor were we invalidating Andrea's vision and years of hard work. We were responding to the fact that we had changed and grown, and we each had evolving needs. Also, as we each grew to "own" a place in the group, we wanted to contribute our unique perspective and shape the future.

In Andrea's hurt, I saw a mirror of my own hurt surrounding the Duquesne Coach Certification Program. I formulated a vision for the program and worked long, hard hours to see that vision come to reality. I succeeded in creating something I believed was good. Students flocked to the program. I expressed that I wanted my role in the program to change, that it was time for new leadership. Yet, when the new leaders took me at my word and began to "own" the program and change it, I felt betrayed and pushed out.

This Wild Women trip provided an unexpected bonus. It reminded me that change in the coach certification program was neither a betrayal nor an invalidation of my work. Life evolves, and I must be ready to let go of sole ownership of my project. My baby will survive without me, and chances are it will even get better along the way. I decided to be thankful for my part in the inception of the program and let others take it to the next step. Obviously, stepping down isn't always the right response to change, but neither is stubbornly suppressing the natural evolution of life.

> *And that's how change happens. One gesture, one person, one moment at a time.*
>
>   ~ Libba Bray

PRINCIPLES TO PROPEL YOU FORWARD

1. In the natural evolution of life, even the best things change.
2. Holding on to "the way things have always been" stifles health and growth.
3. Your greatest strength, overused, is a liability.

FROM MY LIFE TO YOURS

It's natural to resist change, particularly when we are proud of an accomplishment or facing a change in an aspect of life we have treasured.

Resistance to change can come in big areas, like shifting responsibility for something we created, to facing retirement, to seeing a child leave the nest. The resistance can also come in small areas, like a change in how the family celebrates Thanksgiving or the arrangement of the office workroom.

In any case, change is inevitable, and we need to embrace it (or at least accept it) if we want to live large. While change is inevitable, it is not necessarily negative, as letting go makes space for new things, new routines, and new adventures.

Even as change opens the way to new possibilities, it shouldn't be allowed to derail you from your life purpose. Your life purpose should always be your guiding light. I was so happy with the conversation about each woman's life purpose—until it was my turn to speak. I loved facilitating the conversation, drawing out the deep feelings of each participant—until it was my turn. Then I choked up. With the spotlight on my deepest feelings about purpose, I felt shy and embarrassed.

As the women turned the tide and insisted I share my own purpose, I realized I had been hiding behind my own strength of facilitating conversations.

In her book, *Play to Your Strengths*, Andrea Sigetich (of Wild Women fame) defines strengths as follows:

> The innate talents and gifts underpin our skills and passions in our work and in our life. The strengths are the base, and the skills are built on top of them. When we work from our true strengths, our work is easy, effortless—and magnificent.

Identifying and using our strengths, as opposed to fretting about our weaknesses, is part of the process of moving toward a full life. However, there is also the danger of strength overuse. Sometimes, as a defense mechanism, I go into overtime with my strengths. I have great visions for programs and projects but can't muster up the oomph to get them into action. I use my power of being a deep listener to avoid talking about and/or thinking about myself. And my love of connecting people is sometimes a barrier to the self-reflection that I need for balance.

EXERCISE #1: TAKE A LOOK AT YOUR STRENGTHS

1. Write about your feelings surrounding your strengths. Do you know what they are? Do you focus on using strengths or berating yourself for weaknesses?

2. Next, make a list of your strengths. If you have trouble doing this, start by listing your accomplishments. Then work backwards to the strengths that allowed you to succeed.

3. You might consider using an assessment developed by Marcus Buckingham:
   www.tmbc.com/store/standout-assessment.

4. You might also consider Andrea Sigetich's book, *Play to Your Strengths*:
   www.sagecoach.com/leaderstrengths/home.htm.

5. Reflect on any tendency to hide behind your strengths. What are your behaviors when you overuse your strengths?

EXERCISE #2: EXPLORE YOUR FEELINGS ABOUT CHANGE AND CONTROL

1. Write about your attitudes and responses to change. Where in your life are you resisting change? How is the resistance holding you back?

2. Write about your feelings surrounding control. Where in your life are you holding on to control? How is this behavior holding you back?

CHAPTER 14

END OF THE LONG GOODBYE

> *What we have done for ourselves alone dies with us; what we have done for others and the world remains and is immortal.*
>
> ~ Albert Pike

VISITING DON AT SHERWOOD OAKS was like sitting with the ghost of the man I had been married to for 42 years. In moments of quiet, I remembered the reasons I had chosen this older man to be my life partner.

In our early years together, Don wrote poems on napkins, enjoyed candlelight dinners, and was fond of embellishing his conversations with quotes from the classics, often in Latin. Don would tell me the page number and on which side of the page each quote was located. Then he would go to his beloved books in our large library and open to the particular page of the particular book. He was always right.

Don was a perfectionist with a photographic memory and logical mind. He excelled in debate. That combination certainly made our lives at home interesting.

For all my struggles with Don, I never doubted he loved his family. While Don may have been dominant and argumentative, he was steadfastly loyal to Jamie and me as well as to family members from his first marriage. As much as I often wanted to distance myself from Don, I relied on him as an anchor of love and commitment.

With our new living arrangements and the changes I made, I reached the point where I could spend time with Don without anger or resentment. I moved on successfully with life while at the same time spending quality and peaceful time with my husband. There were no more explosive or smoldering emotions. There was, however, frustration as Don often told me to leave, that he didn't want me with him. After making the 30-minute drive from my townhouse to Sherwood Oaks, I'd turn around and make the reverse drive.

I was content with my situation because I was living as I chose. Meanwhile, I was engaged in the task of reconciling my dual life of caring for Don while enjoying unique adventures with Glenn, the new man in my life.

Glenn fit the standards I established when writing a profile for eHarmony. We built a relationship enjoying The Pittsburgh Symphony and attending plays in Pittsburgh and the surrounding region. I even persuaded Glenn to attend two operas with me, something he said he'd never do.

In return, Glenn introduced me to a wonderful group of his friends called the Renegades. Talk about expanding my horizons! Not only did I hike in the mountains with my Wild Women friends, I now began to experience weekend canoeing and tent camping trips on various lakes and rivers.

Here's an example: On a trip to the Grand Canyon of Pennsylvania, we planned to canoe the 18-mile Pine Creek River Gorge, which included one tricky rapid. As we'd been out several times in the canoe already, I felt comfortable paddling in tandem with Glenn. I was totally comfortable in his ability to read the river and rapids. Together, we viewed both the north and south parts of the rapid and decided to take the easier of the two.

When we headed down the north side of the rapid, I was a bit nervous but mostly exhilarated. We made it through the rough part, and I turned to tell Glenn, "That was fun. Let's turn around, go back, and ride the harder of the rapids."

Before the words were out of my mouth, however, we hit a current where the two rapids merged. The boat swirled, turned, and before I knew what hit me, Glenn and I were both in the water.

The next few minutes felt like hours as I was under the boat, under the water, hit on the head by the boat, hit in the back by rocks, and engaged in a desperate fight to keep afloat. Finally, I lost my grip on the boat and headed helplessly downstream until I latched onto a blessed rock and waited to be rescued.

By the time Glenn and I were both safely back in the boat, I had lost a precious earring, one of Glenn's paddles, and my dignity. At that point, we had completed 1 mile of our 18-mile paddle. I don't regret a single moment. I had come a long way from my first solo kayak trip on the Clarion River several years earlier.

This kayak trip is one example of the adventures I shared with Glenn while being present for Don in his diminished state. Around the time of the trip, the husband to Don's granddaughter (mine through marriage) said, "Your grandma is one crazy lady. Why doesn't she slow down like other grandmothers?"

Not this woman, not now. I was (and am) living my dream.

I was also living my dream in my townhouse, enjoying the home I had established based on my vision more than 15 years earlier. I filled the home with books, music, laughter, and invited people to come and stay as long as they needed or wanted.

At one point, while Don was still at Sherwood Oaks, Jamie asked to hold Thanksgiving at my home. He wanted to invite his friends. This was special because for many years our home had been barren at holidays. Don did not like company or family visiting, so the holidays were times of quiet, which sent Jamie elsewhere when most people came home.

Bringing his friends to my home for Thanksgiving was one of the greatest gifts my son has ever given me. The house was filled to the brim with people, noise, laughter, good food, and positive energy. Life felt so full that day.

Soon after that Thanksgiving meal, Jamie and I had to move Don, fighting and screaming, into personal care at Sherwood Oaks. He simply needed more support and daily care. This was the beginning of the end for Don, who on the one hand wanted to die and on the other hand fought hard to stay alive. Once again, we downsized Don's belongings and moved him. This new arrangement did nothing for his already curmudgeonly demeanor.

For the next several months, I carefully balanced my life of fun times with Glenn, peaceful times at home, and even more driving time to visit Don, only to have him treat me with disrespect and/or tell me he didn't want me around. By May of 2012, my energy level was sapped, and my health was once again beginning to wane.

As in the past, Jamie and I were planning trips in the midst of uncertainty surrounding Don's health. As Don declined, Jamie was planning a mountain climbing trip for that July. He planned to summit Mt. Rainier and Mt. Adams with four other climbers. At the same time, Glenn and I were planning a three-week trip to remote national parks in Alaska: Denali, Kenai Fjords, Lake Clark, and Wrangell-St. Elias. Not typical tourists, we planned to make this trip by Alaska Railroad, floatplanes, bush planes, kayak, raft, car, and pontoon boats, into the remotest parts of these parks.

For years, Jamie and I had kept our commitment to each other to avoid putting our lives on hold during Don's long and exhausting illnesses. It had been hard before, and it was hard now. Jamie and I were concerned for Don and wanted to be there for him. We also knew Don's needs could destroy our health and sense of well-being if we allowed them to.

Jamie and I had a heart-to-heart conversation about our plans. We decided that if Don was still alive as the time approached for either of our trips, we would complete our trips. If Don died during the midst of either trip, whoever was home would take care of the funeral arrangements. We would then have a memorial service when the other returned.

When I told Don about this decision, he got a big smile on his face and said, "Absolutely, yes. I want you to enjoy your lives and your adventures." Two weeks later, Don died, before either trip. What a lovely gift he gave us. Because of his generosity, we could continue our lives and live our passions.

Don's funeral was a tribute to his life. For his eulogy, I shared with the many people who attended both the positive and the not-so-positive sides of Don.

Because he was a veteran, Don was eligible for and received a military ceremony. His granddaughter, Laura, and her husband, Josh, are both Marines. Josh was in full military attire and standing at attention during this part of the service. Their son, Jaymes, Don's great-grandson, said to his mom, "What are they doing?"

She answered, "We are saying good-bye to Grampa," and the little boy began to wave at the flag.

He yelled out "Bye, Grampa. Bye, Grampa." What a lovely send off.

I was surprised at how deeply I grieved for Don. With his extended dying, I thought I had grieved in advance. I had considered myself a widow in a practical, if not a legal, sense. I found I was wrong. Don was my husband of 42 years and the anchor of enduring love in my life. I still grieve over the loss.

> *All of us grow up in particular realities—a home,*
> *a family, a clan, a small town, a neighborhood.*
> *Depending upon how we're brought up, we are either*
> *deeply aware of the particular reading of reality into*
> *which we are born, or we are peripherally aware of it.*
> ~ Chaim Potok

PRINCIPLES TO PROPEL YOU FORWARD

1. In the complicated web of family relationships, it is important to balance your own needs with those of others.

2. You'll be most satisfied with yourself when you choose the values that direct your behavior toward family members.

3. Those who bring love and positive attributes into your life deserve your gratitude.

FROM MY LIFE TO YOURS

Family relationships are complicated, full of mixed up emotions and loyalties. For many years, I considered Don a toxic presence in my life, and yet I made a concentrated effort to be loyal to him.

I could have left Don at any time; instead, I created a complicated web, trying to honor Don while creating distance at the same time. While I was by no means perfect at it, I tried to live out my values about marriage. These were values I chose, not those imposed upon me by others.

Although life with Don was difficult, I had a level of contentment because I consistently asserted my right to life as I chose, even when I sacrificed for Don. Even so, it wasn't until Don died that I realized how much his love served as an anchor for me, even as his daily behavior alienated me. As much as Don's personality and needs pulled me back from living the adventurous life I wanted, the anchor of his love was a platform from which I could move safely forward. He deserved my gratitude for 42 years of love.

At the conclusion of my first trip after Don's death, I stepped off the plane and realized I was eager to tell Don all about my adventure. I stepped off the plane wanting to show Don the photos. As I became aware that this was no longer possible, I realized how much the loss of Don meant to me.

Every family relationship is full of contradictions: parent to child, one sibling to another, life partner to life partner, stepparent to child, etc. Each relationship comes with its difficulties, its blessings, and its curses.

We consider some of our relationships life giving and others toxic. Most, however, are a mixed bag. Only our values, our sense of ethics, and the commitments we make to others and ourselves can guide us in these relationships.

EXERCISE #1: FAMILY MATTERS

Write about your values surrounding family.

1. Identify your assumptions about loyalty within a family. What do family members owe each other?

2. Identify the source of these assumptions and values.

3. Have you consciously chosen your values toward family or accepted ones you were taught as a child?

EXERCISE #2: IDENTIFY YOUR BALANCE

Reflect on the significant relationships you have with family members or long-time friends.

1. In each relationship, how do you balance the needs and preferences of the other with your own?

2. In each relationship, what positives are you receiving?

3. What negatives?

4. To what extent are you satisfied with the way you are asserting your right to live as you choose?

5. What changes would make your relationships healthier?

EXERCISE #3: EXPRESS GRATITUDE

In light of the positives you receive in relationships with family members and significant friendships, reflect on how you typically communicate.

1. How would you describe the balance between your expressing appreciation and complaints?

2. What changes are appropriate?

CHAPTER 15

CERTAINTIES AND UNCERTAINTIES

> *Life is full of surprises and serendipity. Being open to unexpected turns in the road is an important part of success. If you try to plan every step, you may miss those wonderful twists and turns. Just find your next adventure—do it well, enjoy it—and then, not now, think about what comes next.*
>
> ~ Condoleezza Rice

DURING MY RECENT TRIP TO ALASKA WITH GLENN, I decided to paraglide off the side of a 2000 foot mount at Aleyeska Mountain Resort within Kenai Fjords National Park. Talk about living large.

I was petrified when the instructor said, "Start running, and don't stop when you get to the edge of the mountain." I trusted myself, ran like hell off the cliff, and had an amazing flying experience on the winds. Glenn was at the landing site to take my picture as I came in.

It meant a great deal to me to experience another adventure and conquer another fear. I've come a long way since I feared walking to the end of the boulder at The Grand Canyon.

With Don gone and his funeral behind us, I am in a new phase of life. With the caregiving persona no longer part of me after more than a decade, I am once again treading water and trying to figure out what is next. Here is what I know:

- I have learned what it is like to be retired from the Duquesne Coach Certification Program and am now comfortable saying I was the co-founder and architect and am now retired from the program.

- I know unequivocally the person I am, what I am capable of doing—or not doing—and I am secure in telling anyone who asks what I am all about.

- I know there is no fear I cannot leap across. I am not afraid to leap off a metaphorical cliff because I know I will fly into new territory successfully. And if my flight isn't successful, I'll learn some valuable life lesson that will make me a better, stronger person.

- I know my legacy to women of my generation is to be a role model by telling my stories. I trust my stories will remind people that they too can step through their fears into living their own particular dreams and passions, no matter what their age or their current circumstances. I hope to shine for women as Frankie did for me on the Isle of Iona. I want to demonstrate that age is not a restrictor unless we allow it to be so.

- I know that, as Joan Anderson says to all her readers, I am "as unfinished as the sea." I have embraced that moniker, Joan, and I'm okay with that.

- I am proud of how I stayed true to my commitment and dedication to my marriage and to helping Don through his trying years into his passing on.

Of course, with every known thought, there is the opposite, the unknown. As a coach, here are the questions I am curious about and will watch to see the answers evolve:

- How will my semi-retirement now define me? How will I keep myself from that horrible fear I've always had of fading into oblivion?

- What does the future hold for my still-young relationship with Glenn?

- What is my next unique adventure? Will I undertake another major project? For example, will I pursue a position in the Peace Corps as I have longed to do? Or will the next phase of my life be marked by a group of calmer, smoother, smaller adventures?

Whatever life holds for me, I will embrace the themes that have made up this book. I will strive to identify and test the assumptions I make, discard ones that no longer apply, and embrace those that test true. I will seek to face my fears with courage, step through with spirit and laughter, and see what becomes clear on the other side. I will play large, no matter how big or small the adventure. I will be true to my passions, no matter the obstacles.

May you also be true to yours.

> *All life is an experiment. The more experiments you make the better.*
>
> ~ Ralph Waldo Emerson

PRINCIPLES TO PROPEL YOU FORWARD

1. As you grow in life, you can build on the self-knowledge you've gained along the way.

2. No matter how much you grow, you will always be unfinished. Embrace the adventure of discovering what comes next.

FROM MY LIFE TO YOURS

In my younger years, I lived on a roller coaster ride of work, caregiving, self-pity, and boredom. I bemoaned how I was becoming a woman 19 years older than my biological age. I felt that I was missing so much of life because of my marriage to a much older man.

While in Toronto, taking courses to become a professional coach, I had an "aha moment" that significantly changed my perspective. I saw a play called "Mamma Mia," featuring the songs of Abba, a Swedish pop group formed in Stockholm in 1972. While sitting alone and listening to that wonderful music of the 70s, I realized that I had never heard of Abba. I wondered what else was missing in my life because of my sheltered role married to someone 19 years older than I. Because of Don's declining health, I was missing my own generation's life happenings. That moment of realization was the start of my deep introspection of what I was doing, testing my assumptions, and making changes that led me to where I am today.

Of course, my trips to Nicaragua and then Machu Picchu were the experiences that propelled me forward with the greatest force. When I began to tell the stories of those and other adventures, students, clients, and others began to tell me, "Donna, if you are taking major risks at your age, then I can do something about my life situation." And they did exactly that.

Eventually my clients, colleagues, and peers asked me to write about my inspirational experiences. Even so, my reticence to talk about my own life delayed the process for a number of years. I felt shy and reluctant to put my story out there. I was worried that the book wouldn't be "good enough" and would somehow embarrass me. Finally, I realized that if I wanted to live my passion of helping women step into their power, I had to share the story of how I stepped into mine.

Writing this book has been cathartic in so many ways. Most importantly, it has shown me that even at the ripe old age of 72, my life is just starting. I still have so many things I want to experience and, as long as my health allows, I will live each moment fully.

After all, if not now, when?

EXERCISE #1: REFLECTION

Reflect on what you have learned about yourself as you've read this book.

1. Which of my stories or struggles resonates most with you?
2. Which principles do you most want to live by?

EXERCISE #2: PASSION AND PURPOSE

Now that you have completed the book and the exercises, describe your passion.

1. Describe how you envision living your passion and purpose from now on.
2. Revisit the vision story you created in Chapter 3. What changes, if any, would you like to make to that story?

EXERCISE #3: YOUR ONE THING

As you come to the end this book, choose one thing you will START doing today that will move you closer to realizing your vision. Choose one thing you will STOP doing today that will change your life.

Describe what you will miss if you do absolutely nothing. Make a commitment to live your own vision. This is the greatest gift you can give to yourself and to the world.

When you were born

You cried

And the world rejoiced.

Live your life so that

When you die

The world cries and you rejoice.

You can hear this lovely Navajo blessing on the album

While You're Alive by Barbara McAfee

ABOUT THE AUTHOR

When not hiking in Costa Rica, Alaska, or the Grand Canyon and living out her vision of unique travel experiences, Donna Billings is helping others fulfill their visions. A certified professional coach and university instructor, Donna uses her extensive training and leadership experience to help professionals reach new levels.

Donna was the architect and co-founder of Duquesne University's Professional Coach Certification Program, an International Coach Federation (ICF) accredited coach certification training program. This program was designed for boomers and re-wired retirees to become either internal or external coach-consultants to upcoming generations. For this work, Donna won the 2013 Innovator Coach of the Year Award from the ICF-Midwest chapters.

Donna coached United Nations leaders as an invited participant in a joint program of the ICF and the United Nations UNICEF and World Food Programme.

In the corporate sector, Donna led a team at a Fortune 500 company in the design, development, and implementation of a highly effective executive leadership assessment and development process targeted for senior management. This program won an award for innovation in learning and development.

Donna's certifications include CPPC through the Coach Training Institute, Professional Certified Coach (PCC) through the International Coach Federation (ICF), and Behavioral Coach through Marshall Goldsmith. She is an authorized facilitator for Team Coaching International; trained in Organizational Relationship Systems Coaching; and a master certification trainer for the Center for Leadership Studies. She has served on the ICF Research and Education Committee and is past president of the Pittsburgh Coaches Association. Donna earned her Master's Degree in Business Education from Robert Morris University.

Donna currently lives in Pittsburgh with her wonderful male companion, Magoo (a miniature schnauzer), and is already planning new unique adventures.

WHAT'S NEXT FOR YOU?

We all climb many mountains over the course of our lives—some are physical, some are mental, some are emotional. Sometimes we are successful. Sometimes we are not. Through coaching, I can help you reach powerful new heights as you traverse whatever life transition you're now experiencing.

Life changes are challenging, scary—and exciting. Let's talk if you are ready to transition into a new career, shift gears into a meaningful re-wired retirement, or take action to change your life. Together we'll design the next stage of your life to be successful and satisfying.

I invite you to attend a *New Beginnings Retreat for Women and "Boomers" in Transition*. In addition, your organization may want to schedule a *Managing and Coaching across Generations* workshop.

To learn more, contact me through one of the following websites:

- www.DonnaBillingsCoach.com
- www.RedAndPurpleHikingBoots.com

SUGGESTED READING

Anderson, J. (1999). A year by the sea: thoughts of an unfinished woman. New York: Broadway Books. Also go to
www.joanandersononline.com for a list of Joan's other books
and retreats.

Bridges, W. (2004). Transitions: making sense of life's changes.
Jackson: TN: Da Capo Press.

Carson, R. (2003). Taming your gremlin: a surprisingly simple
method for getting out of your own way. New York: William
Morrow Paperbacks.

Hollis, J. (1993). The middle passage from misery to meaning in
midlife. Toronto: Inner City Books.

Joseph, J. (2001). Warning: When I am an old woman I shall
wear purple. London: Souvenir Press.

Martz, S. (Ed.). (2007). When I am old I shall wear purple (4th
ed.). Watsonville, CA: Papier MacHe.

Sigetich, A. & Leavitt, C. (2007). Play to your strengths: stacking
the deck to achieve spectacular results for yourself and others. Pompton Plains, NJ: Career Press.